Migrating from Drupal to Backdrop

Todd Tomlinson

Apress®

Migrating from Drupal to Backdrop

ISBN-13 (pbk): 978-1-4842-1759-7

ISBN-13 (electronic): 978-1-4842-1760-3

Managing Director: Welmoed Spahr
Lead Editor: Ben Renow-Clarke
Technical Reviewer: Eric Goldman
Editorial Board: Steve Anglin, Pramila Balin, Louise Corrigan, James DeWolf, Jonathan Gennick, Robert Hutchinson, Celestin Suresh John, Michelle Lowman, James Markham, Susan McDermott, Matthew Moodie, Jeffrey Pepper, Douglas Pundick, Ben Renow-Clarke, Gwenan Spearing
Coordinating Editor: Melissa Maldonado
Copy Editor: Kim Wimpsett
Compositor: SPi Global
Indexer: SPi Global

Distributed to the book trade worldwide by Springer Science+Business Media New York, 233 Spring Street, 6th Floor, New York, NY 10013. Phone 1-800-SPRINGER, fax (201) 348-4505, e-mail orders-ny@springer-sbm.com, or visit www.springer.com. Apress Media, LLC is a California LLC and the sole member (owner) is Springer Science + Business Media Finance Inc (SSBM Finance Inc). SSBM Finance Inc is a Delaware corporation.

For information on translations, please e-mail rights@apress.com, or visit www.apress.com.

Apress and friends of ED books may be purchased in bulk for academic, corporate, or promotional use. eBook versions and licenses are also available for most titles. For more information, reference our Special Bulk Sales–eBook Licensing web page at www.apress.com/bulk-sales.

Any source code or other supplementary materials referenced by the author in this text is available to readers at www.apress.com. For detailed information about how to locate your book's source code, go to www.apress.com/source-code/.

There are so many people to thank for making this book possible, including dozens of very special people who had a huge influence on my life and my desire to write. This book is dedicated to them.

To my wife, Misty, who consistently sacrifices time together to allow me to pursue my dream of writing. Thank you for always standing beside me and for always encouraging and supporting me. I love you more.

To my daughters, Anna, Emma, and Alissa, for allowing Dad to write when you'd really rather be out doing something fun.

To my parents for giving me so many opportunities to explore my dreams and desires. Without your support and encouragement none of this would be possible.

I want to especially thank my grandmother, Gladys Tomlinson, who passed away a year ago at age 102. She authored and published her first book at age 96. Thank you, Grandma, for all you've done for me over the years, for the influence that you have had on my life, and for inspiring me to write.

And to Eric Goldman for stepping in as the technical reviewer of this book. You jumped into the deep end of the pool with both feet and without a life preserver and you did it! Thank you for catching the subtle nuances and for making this book great!

Contents at a Glance

Contents

About the Author

Todd Tomlinson is the senior enterprise Drupal architect and senior Drupal developer at Danaher Corporation, a $22 billion high-tech manufacturing company. Todd's focus over the past 20 years has been on designing, developing, deploying, and supporting complex web solutions for public- and private-sector clients all around the world. He has been using Drupal as the primary platform for creating beautiful and feature-rich sites since Drupal 4. Todd is also the author of *Beginning Drupal 7* (Apress), *Pro Drupal 7 Development* (Apress), and *Beginning Drupal 8* (Apress).

Prior to joining Danaher, Todd was the vice president of ServerLogic's national Drupal consulting practice and senior director of eBusiness Strategic Services for Oracle Corporation, where he helped Oracle's largest clients develop their strategic plans for leveraging the Web as a core component of their business. He was also the former vice president of Internet solutions for Claremont Technology Group, the vice president and CTO of Emerald Solutions, a senior enterprise Drupal architect at Unicon, the managing director for CNF Ventures, and a senior manager with Andersen Consulting/Accenture.

Todd has a BS in computer science, an MBA, and a PhD (ABD).

Todd's passion for Drupal is evident in his obsession with evangelizing the platform and his enthusiasm when speaking with clients about the possibilities of what they can accomplish using Drupal. If you want to see someone light up, stop him on the street and ask him, "What is Drupal, and what can it do for me?"

About the Technical Reviewer

Eric Goldman is a technical project manager for a Open Source software development consultancy in Gilbert, AZ. He holds a BS in managerial economics from the University of Massachusetts and has been involved in the IT industry for 25+ years. He has worked for various companies such as BBN, American Express, and Charles Schwab. He has held project manager, web developer/admin, consultant, and director of IT roles. Eric has been part of the Web since its early day; he discovered Drupal three years ago and has been immersing himself in all its glory ever since. He is currently working on updating/upgrading a nonprofit Land Trust Site to Backdrop.

When not at work, Eric likes to spend time with his family, goes camping, is an avid reader, and is pursuing his newest hobby, photographing the night skies.

Acknowledgments

In addition to the family and friends that I dedicated my book to, I would like to thank the following people:

My in-laws, Donna and Dick, for believing in me and for sharing their amazing daughter with me.

My sisters for putting up with a geeky brother, before geeky was cool.

The Apress team for leading me through the jungle of authoring a book. Without your passion for publishing the best books on the planet, I wouldn't have had the opportunity to cross the "author a book" item off my bucket list.

Introduction

In its relatively short life, Drupal has had a tremendous impact on the landscape of the Internet. As a web content management system (CMS), Drupal has enabled the creation of feature- and content-rich web sites for organizations large and small. With the release of Drupal 8 and the shift in focus toward large-scale enterprise solutions and the re-platforming of Drupal on Symfony, small to medium-sized organizations are faced with choosing one of the following:

- Bite the bullet and build or acquire the skills necessary to fully embrace Drupal 8

- Stay on Drupal 6 or 7, knowing that they will be unsupported in the future

- Migrate to another CMS

- Leverage their investment in Drupal 7 by moving to Backdrop, a "cousin" of Drupal that utilizes the same underlying architecture as Drupal 7

This book will help those who are faced with the decision on which direction to take and demonstrates the relative simplicity of moving from Drupal 7 to Backdrop. I'll walk you through the process of porting modules, themes, and page layouts. I'll also demonstrate the differences in the administrative interfaces and show where to find and how to install Backdrop core, contributed modules, and themes. I'll also cover how to contribute to the Backdrop community.

Like with all open source projects, Backdrop is constantly evolving. Check the Backdrop web site, http://backdropcms.org, for the latest information on the platform, as well as the errata for this book posted on Apress.com.

■ ■ ■

## CHAPTER 1

Introduction to Backdrop

Backdrop (https://backdropcms.org/) is a web content management system with its roots deeply intertwined with Drupal, the market-leading open source web content management system. Backdrop was created by a team who believed the focus of Drupal was shifting toward a platform tailored for large-scale enterprise, leaving behind the thousands of nonprofits, small to medium-sized businesses, educational institutions, and organizations that are delivering comprehensive web sites on a budget. If you are in one of those organizations that has an investment in Drupal 6 or 7 and are weighing your options of migrating to Drupal 8 or looking for alternatives such as Backdrop, then this book was written for you. Backdrop promises to deliver a familiar solution that is less complex than Drupal 8 and is based on the foundation of Drupal that thousands of developers have experience with.

The Backdrop Organization's Goals

The founders of Backdrop set out with a goal of improving and simplifying the code and architecture of Drupal, making it even easier for smaller organizations to build robust and feature-rich web solutions without the complexities and learning curve associated with Drupal 8 and its move to Symfony. There is also a focus on site builders, those who use the administrative interface in Drupal to construct sites. Drupal's focus has been on the developer community, and for small to medium-sized organizations, maintaining a development team to support ongoing site development and management activities is often cost prohibitive.

Affordability

Affordability is a common thread throughout the vision and mission of the Backdrop organization, including making Backdrop less resource intensive than Drupal 8, providing organizations with a solution that can be supported on shared hosting environments such as Go Daddy.

1

Core Principles

The creators of Backdrop defined a set of core principles, some of which diverge from the Drupal community but are important to understand when evaluating a move to Backdrop.

- *Make backward compatibility important*: Backdrop will attempt to keep API changes to a minimum so that contributed code can be maintained easily and existing sites can be updated affordably. Every big change that can't be made backward compatible will need to be carefully considered and measured against Backdrop's other principles. For those who have lived through migrating sites from Drupal 4 to 5, 5 to 6, 6 to 7, and now 7 to 8, the pain of change is often the greatest deterrent to migrating from one major version to another. The Backdrop team understands this dilemma and is addressing it with a focus on backward compatibility.

- *Write code for the majority*. Backdrop's aim is to be easy to learn and build upon, even for those with a minimal amount of technical knowledge. The underlying philosophy is to focus on the site builders instead of the developers, making site building as easy as possible and making how things work immediately clear and easily documentable.

- *Include features for the majority*: The team's directive is that core should include only the features and tools that benefit the majority of sites that are running on it, keeping the complexity and footprint of core to a minimum. This approach is central to the focus on making Backdrop friendly to the shared hosting providers, keeping the costs of hosting a Backdrop site low.

- *Ensure that Backdrop can be extended*: With a focus on keeping core to a minimal footprint, ensuring that Backdrop may be extended through contributed modules is critical. Complex solutions will be relegated to contributed modules as will use cases that are too specific to be considered as candidates for core.

- *Meet low system requirements*: Backdrop must be able to run on affordable hosting with basic requirements, foregoing popular trends in technology over common, proven, and learnable systems.

- *Plan and schedule releases*: Each release will contain a set of features and will be released on time. If a feature is not ready in time for a specific release, the feature will be postponed so the release will still be delivered on time.

- *Remain free and open source*: Open source has the ability to change the world for the better. All code included with Backdrop is under an open source license that allows anyone to use it free of charge, regardless of their beliefs or intentions.

While many of these principles are similar to Drupal, there are subtle differences that focus on meeting the needs and budgets of small to medium-sized organizations and on making the adoption and continued use of Backdrop as an organization's content management system (CMS) less complex, painful, and costly.

Key Differences Between Drupal and Backdrop

While the foundation of Backdrop is Drupal, this book will discuss several key differences. The following are the key ones you should keep in mind as you read this book:

- You can't take a Drupal 7 module and just install it on Backdrop without some modification. In Chapter 5, I'll cover common changes that must be made to a Drupal 7 module to make it compatible with Backdrop. Some of the changes are simple, such as editing the module's .info file and changing core = 7.x to backdrop = 1.x.

- Backdrop uses configuration management instead of variables that are stored in the database. Backdrop adopted the Drupal 8 approach of moving configuration information out of the database and into the file system, making it easier to manage the process of deploying code and configuration between environments. In Chapter 5, I'll cover how to change a Drupal 7 module to accommodate how Backdrop handles configuration.

- The file structure has changed. Common Drupal files such as settings.php and common directories such as the Files directory are now located in the root directory of your site. You'll also notice fewer files in the root directory. In an off-the-shelf installation of Drupal 7, there are 25 files/directories in the root directory, whereas in Backdrop there are only 12. In Chapter 2, I'll cover the differences in the file system and where to find the directories and files that a typical Drupal developer or site builder might use and where they can be found in Backdrop.

- The installation process has changed. The Backdrop team simplified the installation process. In Chapter 2, I'll cover the process of installing Backdrop, highlighting the primary changes between installing Drupal and Backdrop.

- The user interface has changed. While Backdrop looks a lot like Drupal, including Bartik as the default theme, there are key differences in editorial/content management, site building, and site management elements in Backdrop. In Chapter 3, I'll cover what has changed in the administrative and editorial interface in Backdrop.

- The process for locating contributed modules and themes is different from Drupal in that modules and themes are located on GitHub. In Chapter 4, I'll cover the process for finding, downloading, and installing contributed modules and themes in Backdrop.

- Building pages has changed in Backdrop. Panels were ported to Backdrop; however, the administrative interface for creating pages has changed significantly. In Chapter 7, I'll cover the Layout module and how pages are constructed in Backdrop.

With a general understanding of the key differences between Backdrop and Drupal, the next task is to migrate an existing Drupal 6 or Drupal 7 site to Backdrop.

Migrating a Drupal Site to Backdrop

Although it is by no means a trivial task, in Chapter 7 I'll demystify the process of planning for a migration from Drupal 6 to Backdrop and provide a step-by-step guide and demonstration of migrating a Drupal 6 site to Backdrop. In Chapter 8, I'll follow the same process with a focus on migrating a Drupal 7 site to Backdrop.

Summary

A vast majority of the Drupal sites deployed on the Web are for small to medium-sized organizations, nonprofits, and educational institutions that are now faced with the decision of continuing to run their sites on a nonsupported platform (Drupal 6) or undertake the effort to learn a whole new Drupal ecosystem based on Symfony and undertake migrating their sites to Drupal 8. Backdrop represents an alternative foundation for organizations with limited budgets and human resources that leverages an organization's existing investment in Drupal solutions, experience, and skill sets.

In the next chapter, I'll cover the process of installing Backdrop and the changes that you will find in the directory structure and file system, which are the first steps in preparing to migrate your Drupal site to Backdrop.

■ ■ ■

## CHAPTER 2

Installing Backdrop

The process for installing Backdrop is similar to installing Drupal, with a few minor variances. In this chapter, I will walk you through the process of downloading and installing Backdrop. I'll also describe the differences in the directory structure and file system between Backdrop and Drupal. By the end of this chapter, you will have the information necessary to successfully install Backdrop on a shared hosting environment and your local system.

System Requirements

The Backdrop team focused on minimizing the system requirements for Backdrop, making the platform a "shared hosting"–friendly CMS. The following are the base requirements for installing Backdrop:

- PHP 5.3.2 or higher.

- MySQL or MariaDB 5.0.15 or higher (with PDO).

- Apache web server recommended versions 1.3 as well as stable versions 2.*x* hosted on UNIX/Linux, OS X, or Windows. Backdrop is also supported on Nginx (0.7.*x*, 0.8.*x*, 1.0.*x*, 1.2.*x*), stable 1.4.*x* versions, and mainline 1.5.*x* versions hosted on UNIX/Linux, OS X, or Windows.

- A *minimum* of 15 MB of disk space is required to install Backdrop. Additional contributed modules and themes will typically push the requirements to 60 MB of disk space. Additional storage will be required to support images, file attachments, and other media. A good starting point is 250 MB of disk.

Most low-cost commercial shared hosting platforms meet or exceed the minimum requirements for Backdrop.

Downloading Backdrop

You can download Backdrop from the Backdrop web site (https://backdropcms.org) by clicking the Download Backdrop button, or you can clone Backdrop from GitHub (https://github.com/backdrop/backdrop).

Clicking the Download Zip button allows you to download the backdrop.zip file that contains Backdrop's core components. You can move that zip file to the appropriate directory on your web server or shared hosting account and unzip the file. For information on where the backdrop.zip file should reside, check your web server or shared hosting documentation. Typical locations are /var/www/html for Apache and /usr/share/nginx/html for Nginix.

If you prefer using Git (https://git-scm.com/), you can clone the Backdrop core repository by using the following:

```
git clone https://github.com/backdrop/backdrop.git <directory name>
```

Replace <directory name> with the name of the directory where Backdrop will reside.

Installing Backdrop

There are several steps to installing Backdrop on your shared hosting platform, dedicated hosting environment, or local web server. The following are the general steps after downloading Backdrop core to the appropriate directory:

1. Create the database and database user.

2. Set permissions on settings.php and the files directory.

3. Run the Backdrop installation process.

Those who have installed Drupal in the past will be pleasantly surprised at the familiarity of the installation process.

Creating the Database

With Backdrop core copied to your web server's root directory (or appropriate subdirectory for those with multiple sites on a single web server), the next step in the process is to create the MySQL or MariaDB database and database user. Most shared hosting providers will enable this capability through a web-based cPanel or PHPMyAdmin interface; review your hosting provider's documentation for more details on the tools and approach for creating databases and database users.

If you have command-line access to your web server, you can also create the database and user from the command line. For information on how to create databases and users from the command line, visit https://dev.mysql.com/doc.

Using the web-based or command-line tools, follow these steps:

1. Create a database, and make a note of the database name and hostname (usually localhost).

2. Create a database user, and make a note of the username and password.

3. Grant this new user ALL privileges on the database just created.

Setting File Permissions

You can find Backdrop's settings.php file and the files directory in the root directory of your Backdrop installation. You will need to set permissions on both settings.php and the files directory so that your web server can update and write to both the file and the directory.

During installation, the permissions should be set such that the owner of the settings.php file (the web server) has write permissions, but all others have only read permissions. In Linux/Unix/OS X environments, those permissions would be set to 644 (owner read/write, group read, others read). The same settings apply to the files directory.

If you are using a shared or dedicated hosting platform, check your provider's documentation on how to set file permissions. Typically cPanel includes a file manager, which includes the ability to set permissions. Set the value for the owner to 6, the group to 4, and all others to 4. If you have command-line access, you may update the owner of settings.php and the files directory to the user account tied to your web server (in the case of Apache, the default owner for files is _www).

```
sudo chown _www settings.php
sudo chown _www files
```

The second step is to update the permissions so that the web server has write permissions to settings.php and the files directory.

```
chmod u+w settings.php
chmod u+w files
```

Running the Backdrop Installer

With Backdrop core residing in the proper web server directory, the database created, and the file and directory permissions set correctly, you are now ready to run the installer. Visit your site using http://<url of your site>, and you should see the first step in the installation process, as shown in Figure 2-1.

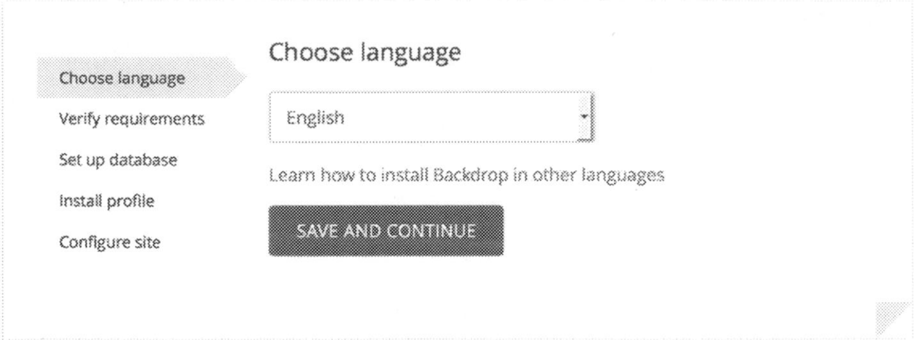

Choose language

Choose language

Verify requirements   English

Set up database

Learn how to install Backdrop in other languages

Install profile

Configure site   SAVE AND CONTINUE

Figure 2-1. *Step 1 in the Backdrop installation process*

Backdrop in late 2015 ships only in English. In the future, other languages may be included as out-of-the-box translations. Click the SAVE AND CONTINUE button to continue the installation process.

The next screen in the process (see Figure 2-2) is where you specify the database name, the database username, and the database user password. There are also optional fields for situations where you are utilizing a remote database for your Backdrop site. Those fields are not required for installations where the database resides on the same server that you are installing Backdrop on and you are using the standard MySQL or MariaDB port and table prefix.

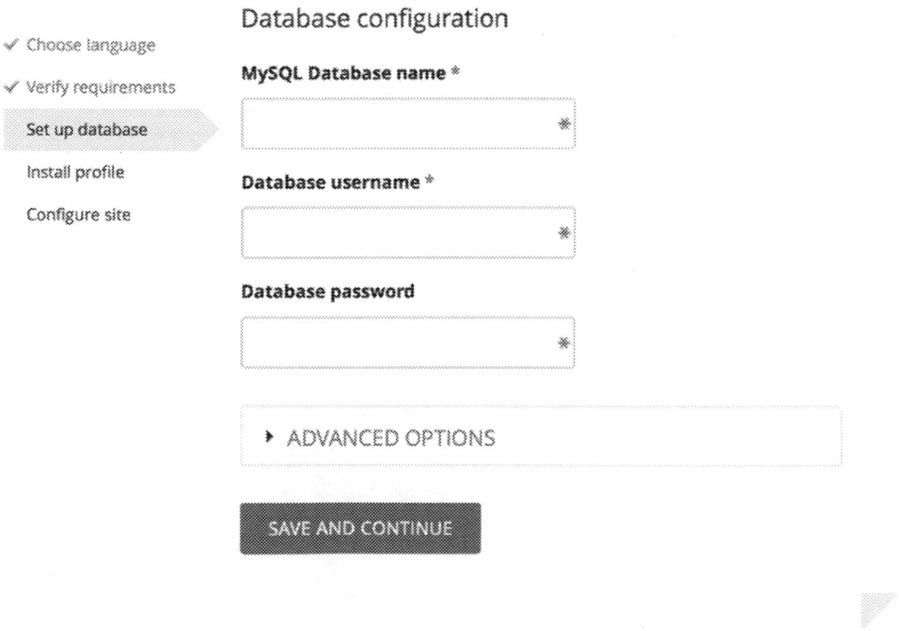

Database configuration

✓ Choose language

✓ Verify requirements

MySQL Database name *

Set up database

Install profile

Database username *

Configure site

Database password

▶ ADVANCED OPTIONS

SAVE AND CONTINUE

Figure 2-2. *Setting the database configuration parameters*

After entering the appropriate values, click the SAVE AND CONTINUE button. Backdrop creates the database tables required for Backdrop core and populates those tables with baseline information.

The final step in the process is to set basic site information values (see Figure 2-3). Enter appropriate values in each field and click the SAVE AND CONTINUE button to complete the installation process.

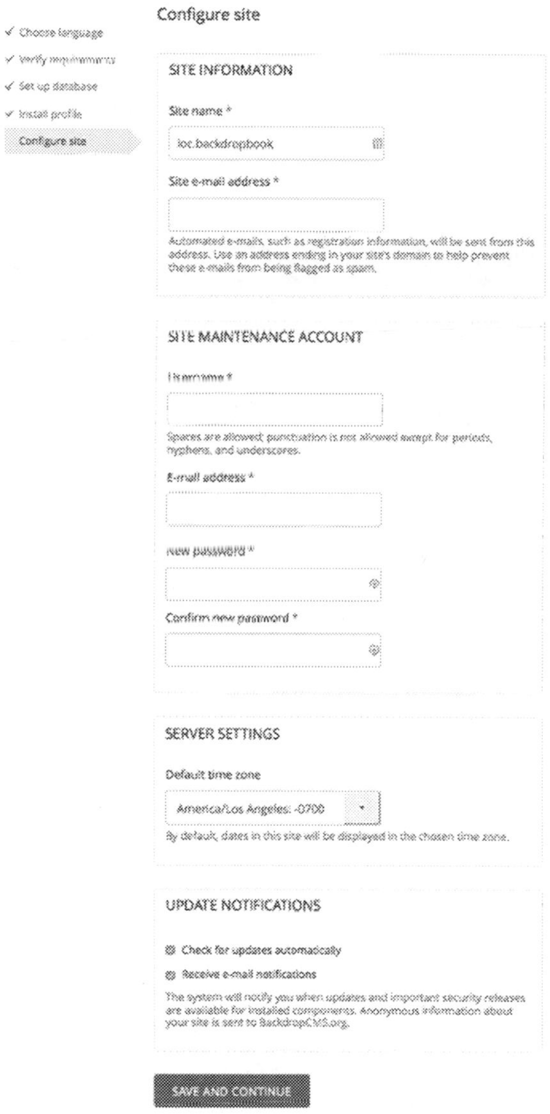

Figure 2-3. *Entering basic site information*

9

After completing the installation process, you are taken to the home page of your new Backdrop site, logged in as the site administrator (see Figure 2-4).

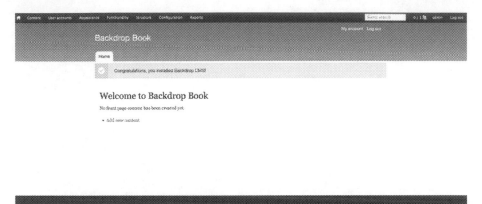

Figure 2-4. *The home page of your new Backdrop site*

File and Directory Structure Differences

After installing Backdrop, you'll notice that there are several key differences in the file system between Backdrop and Drupal 7.

- There are significantly fewer files in the root directory of the site. Drupal 7 has 25 files/directories, whereas Backdrop has only 11.

- The settings.php file and the files directory exist by default in the root directory.

- The installation files update.php, cron.php, and authorize.php and the includes, misc, and scripts directories are in the core subdirectory on Backdrop instead of the root directory (Drupal 7).

- There are several differences in the modules directory, including modules that are present in Drupal 7's core distribution but not in Backdrop, as well as modules in Backdrop that are not part of Drupal 7 core.

- Garland is not included as a core theme.

There are other subtle changes in directories and files; these are the major changes.

Summary

With a focus on small to medium-sized organizations, the principle of simplification is apparent from the start of the installation process through a quick review of the file structure. In the next chapter, I'll cover the major changes to the editorial and administration interface.

CHAPTER 3

∎ ∎ ∎

Editorial and Administration Interface Differences

Backdrop's editorial and administrative interfaces are similar to Drupal with several subtle changes focused on simplifying the process for content editors, site builders, and site administrators. In this chapter, I'll cover the major differences between Backdrop and Drupal 7.

Administrator's Menu Bar

There are several minor differences in the administrator's menu bar between Backdrop and Drupal 7. The administrator's menu bar in Backdrop (see Figure 3-1) is based on the Admin Bar module, which brings several of Drupal 7's contributed module features back into Backdrop core, such as the ability to clear cache directly from the toolbar by clicking the Home icon. Other changes include renaming common menu items such as "People" in Drupal 7 to "User accounts" and such as "Modules" in Drupal 7 to "Functionality."

Figure 3-1. *The administrator's toolbar in Backdrop*

Content

The primary changes in the content administration functionality are that Backdrop has separated comment administration into its own stand-alone page (versus a tab on the content listing page in Drupal 7) and has rearranged the filtering options. The following are the primary changes to the content-authoring interface in Backdrop:

- There's a new WYSIWYG editor in Backdrop core (called CKEditor).
- The vertical tabs for options have been rearranged.
- An option to add a new content item to a menu has been removed.
- The revisions option has been removed.

User Accounts

The administrative interface for creating user accounts in Backdrop is identical to Drupal 7. The user account listing page, accessed in Backdrop by clicking the "User accounts" item in the administrator's menu bar, differs slightly from the Drupal 7 listing page, with the primary differences being the removal of the Permissions tab from the listing page, slight changes in the layout of the filters, and changes in wording on the bulk update feature.

Themes

The administrative interface for themes in Backdrop is virtually identical to Drupal 7, with the primary difference being the removal of Garland as a theme that is included in core. The process for installing, enabling, and configuring themes remains unchanged, with the exception of minor help-text changes.

Modules

As part of the Backdrop team's desire to simplify and reduce the footprint of Backdrop to make it more friendly to lower-cost hosting solutions, the number of modules shipped with Backdrop core is fewer than Drupal 7, removing some of the least frequently used modules from core and adding several contributed modules that everyone used by default. The following are the modules that were removed:

- aggregator
- blog
- dashboard
- forum

- help
- openid
- overlay
- php
- poll
- profile
- rdf
- shortcut
- statistics
- toolbar
- tracker
- trigger

The following are the modules that were added to Backdrop that are not part of Drupal 7 core:

- admin bar (replacement for toolbar)
- ckeditor
- config (configuration management)
- date
- email
- entity
- instantfilter
- language
- layout
- link
- responsive table
- uuid
- views
- views bulk operations
- views_ui

You can find the administrative interface for modules in Backdrop under the Functionality link on the administrator's menu. The interface in Backdrop is similar to Drupal 7, with minor improvements such as providing the ability to search for modules and organizing core modules by functionality rather than just an alphabetical list.

There are additional menu links from the administrator's menu that take you directly to the functionality for downloading a new module, updating modules, and uninstalling modules, whereas in Drupal 7 those were either links or tabs on the module listing page.

The interface for installing, updating, and uninstalling modules is virtually identical in Backdrop and Drupal 7, with minor wording changes in the help text because of the differences in Backdrop and Drupal.

Content Types

Backdrop does away with the Article and Basic Page content types in favor of a Post and Page content type. Both Backdrop content types retain the similar functionality of their Drupal 7 equivalents.

The interface for creating content types remains relatively unchanged (see Figure 3-2); the minor exceptions are as follows:

- The Edit tab in Drupal 7 has become the Configure tab in Backdrop.

- The preview options have been removed from the "Submission form settings" tab.

- On the "Publishing settings" tab, the default state for a content item has been changed to a radio button offering the ability to specifically say that a default state is unpublished (whereas Drupal 7 implied unpublished if the Published checkbox was checked). Also, creating a new revision has been moved to a separate tab named "Revision settings," and there are minor wording changes to the options for making a content item sticky and promoting a content item to the front page of the site.

- Display settings in Backdrop now includes the option to enable author pictures in posts at the content type level instead of globally because Drupal 7 handled user pictures at the theme layer in the theme's administration settings.

- Comment settings have minor label and description changes as well as a new option to enable user pictures in comments at the content type level.

- The "Menu settings" tab lists menus that have been renamed from Drupal 7. The options in Backdrop are Account Menu, Administration Menu, and Primary Navigation.

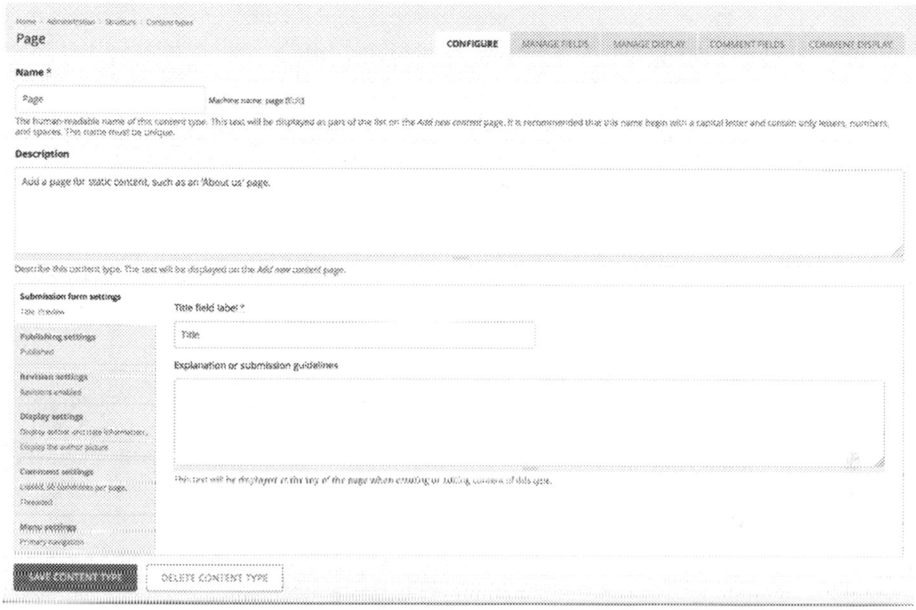

Figure 3-2. *Creating or editing a content type*

The Manage Fields tab includes a new default field on content types, URL Path Settings, because the Path module is included in Backdrop core, whereas it was a contributed module that was not part of Drupal 7 core. Backdrop also provides several field types in core that were available only as contributed modules in Drupal 7. Additional field types include Date, Email, and Link, and there has been a reorganization of numeric fields by grouping integer, float, and decimal with a prefix of Number (see Figure 3-3).

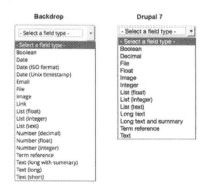

Figure 3-3. *Field types available in Backdrop and Drupal 7 core*

There are minor text changes to the elements included on the "Manage display" tab, and the "Comment fields" tab includes only the Comment body field, whereas Drupal 7 included the "Comment author" and "Comment subject" fields.

Blocks

The administrative interface for blocks is significantly different in Backdrop. Hovering your cursor over the Structure link in the administrator's menu displays a "Custom blocks" link. Clicking "Custom blocks" reveals a page that lists only custom blocks created on this site, not the off-the-shelf blocks provided by Backdrop core. The Backdrop core blocks are displayed only in the administrative interface for creating layouts, which I will cover in Chapter 6.

The process for creating custom blocks has been significantly simplified in Backdrop. The administrative interface, as shown in Figure 3-4, provides only basic information about the block and not the placement or visibility of the block. Those attributes have been moved to the interface associated with adding a block to a layout and is described in Chapter 6.

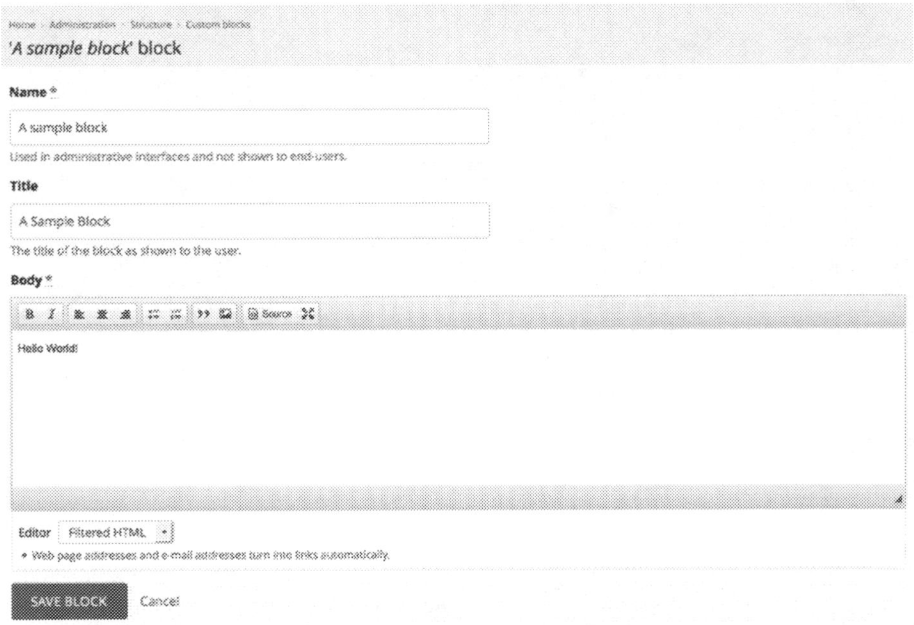

Figure 3-4. *Creating a custom block*

Menus

The administrative interface for creating menus has remained relatively unchanged from Drupal 7 to Backdrop, with the primary changes being the names of the menus. The user menu has been renamed to the account menu, the main menu has been renamed primary menu, the management menu has been renamed to administration menu, and the navigation menu in Drupal 7 has been removed in Backdrop.

Taxonomy

The administrative interface and processes associated with creating vocabularies and terms has remained relatively unchanged. There are minor updates to the placement of elements on the screens and updates to help text.

Views

Backdrop followed Drupal 8's approach of incorporating views into core. There are fewer off-the-shelf views available in Backdrop, following the principle of making things simpler. The interface for creating and administering views remains virtually unchanged from Drupal 7 as a contributed module to views in Backdrop core

Configuration

Clicking the Configuration link in the administrator's menu reveals a list of tasks that have been clarified and focuses on the tasks that site administrators perform (see Figure 3-5). No longer do you have to hunt for the link to update permissions, and options that are rarely used have been removed, such as IP Address Blocking.

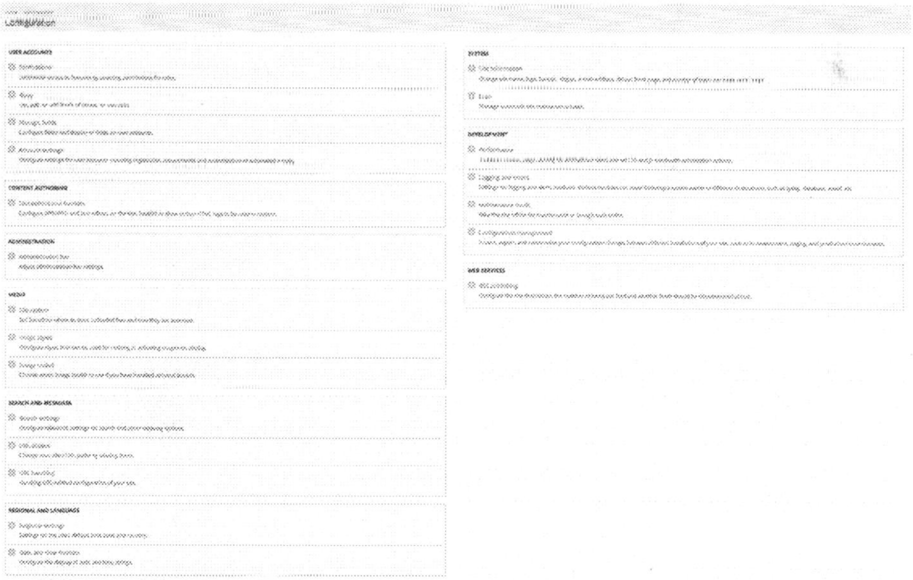

Figure 3-5. *Configuration options*

One of the major changes to Backdrop is the addition of configuration management, which appears as an option in the Development section of the page. I'll cover the use of configuration management in Chapter 5.

Reports

Reports remain virtually unchanged from Drupal 7, with the lone exception of a new report in Backdrop for view plug-ins, which is available by default in Backdrop because of the inclusion of views in core. This report is also available in Drupal 7 but only after downloading and enabling views as a contributed module.

Summary

The Backdrop team's vision of simplifying the overall experience for content editors, site builders, and site administrators is evident in the "cleaner and leaner" interface and functionality described in this chapter. While it has been simplified, Backdrop will be familiar to those who have implemented, administered, and authored content on a Drupal 7 site.

In the next chapter, I'll highlight the changes to the location of contributed modules and themes and the processes for installing and enabling modules in Backdrop.

■ ■ ■

## CHAPTER 4

Backdrop Modules and Themes

While installing and configuring Backdrop modules and themes through the Backdrop administrative interface is nearly identical to Drupal 7, as of now there isn't a fully functional Drush equivalent for Backdrop. The other primary difference is that all of Backdrop core, contributed modules, and themes are hosted on GitHub. In this chapter, I'll cover the differences in installing contributed modules and themes from outside the Backdrop administrative interface.

Locating Backdrop Contributed Modules

The Backdrop team is working on providing the list of available contributed modules and themes on the Backdrop web site, but that capability is rudimentary as of the writing of this book. The list of modules and themes is relatively short, and searching/browsing through the list is the only mechanism on the web site (no filtering by category or release or any sorting capabilities). To view the list, visit https://backdropcms.org/modules.

The official repository of all Backdrop contributed modules and themes is Backdrop's GitHub account, accessible through https://github.com/backdrop-contrib.

You can download contributed modules and themes either by clicking the download link on the Backdrop web site or by visiting the GitHub repository and downloading from there. The advantage of downloading from GitHub is that the GitHub page provides a git clone URL, whereas the web site only provides the ability to download the file through a link.

Downloading Backdrop Modules and Themes

As in Drupal 7, there are two basic ways to upload modules to a Backdrop site; you can download the file from GitHub and place the files on the server in the Modules directory in the root directory of your Backdrop site, or you can use the administrative interface to upload the module. Since the upload through the administrative interface requires that your server is configured properly to handle FTP uploads, I'll briefly cover installing the files by downloading them.

19

You can download the files by clicking the link from the http://Backdropcms.org/ modules page.

YouTube Field

Figure 4-1. *Clicking the download link from the Backdrop web site*

Clicking the link results in a pop-up window that allows you to specify that you want to save the file; save the zip file in the Modules directory. Once the file is in the directory, use an appropriate tool to unzip the contents and then delete the zip file.

To download the file from GitHub via git, you can search for the module on http://github.com/backdrop-contrib. Once you have located the module, you should see a page that looks similar to Figure 4-2.

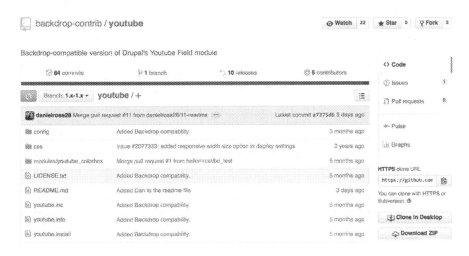

Figure 4-2. *A Backdrop module page on GitHub*

You can click the Download ZIP button located in the right column of the page, or you can use git to clone the files through a terminal window by using git to clone the module's repository in the Modules directory of your site. The benefit of using git is that updates to the module may be pulled by visiting the Modules directory and executing a git pull to download updates to the module.

To clone the module using git, open a terminal window, copy the URL from the HTTPS clone URL field in the right column of the module's GitHub page, and enter a command that follows this structure:

```
git clone <https URL copied from the modules page> <name of the directory
where the module should go>
```

The following example clones the YouTube Field module and places it into a directory named youtube in my site's module directory:

```
$ git clone https://github.com/backdrop-contrib/youtube.git youtube
```

The result I see as git downloads the module is as follows:

```
Cloning into 'youtube'...
remote: Counting objects: 554, done.
remote: Total 554 (delta 0), reused 0 (delta 0), pack-reused 554
Receiving objects: 100% (554/554), 107.79 KiB, done.
Resolving deltas. 100% (288/288), done.
```

Regardless of whether I downloaded the zip file or used git to clone the module from GitHub, the next step is to visit the site while logged in as an administrator and enable the module. In my example, after clicking the Functionality link in the administrator's menu, I'm presented with a list of all the modules. Scrolling down the page, I see the YouTube Field module. Clicking the check box for that module and clicking the Save configuration button at the bottom of the page results in the module being enabled and ready for configuration and use.

	NAME	VERSION	DESCRIPTION
	Email	1.3.x-dev	Defines an email field type.
	Field UI	1.3.x-dev	User interface for the Field API. more
	File	1.3.x-dev	Defines a file field type. more
	Image	1.3.x-dev	Provides image manipulation tools and image field type. more
	Link	1.3.x-dev	Defines simple link field types.
	List	1.3.x-dev	Defines list field types. Use with Options to create selection lists. more
	Number	1.3.x-dev	Defines numeric field types. more
	Options	1.3.x-dev	Defines selection, check box and radio button widgets for text and numeric fields. more
	YouTube Field	1.3.x-dev	Provides a YouTube widget for fields. more
	YouTube Field Colorbox	1.3.x-dev	Provides Colorbox support to YouTube Field thumbnail display settings. more

Figure 4-3. *Enabling the YouTube Field module*

Downloading and enabling themes (http://backdropcms.org/themes) is identical to the process for modules, with the primary exception being that themes are loaded into the Themes directory. To enable a theme, click the Appearance link on the administrator's menu and then click the "Enable and set default" link, as shown in Figure 4-4.

DISABLED THEMES

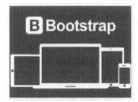

Bootstrap lite 1.x-3.3.5.1

Built to use Bootstrap, a sleek, intuitive, and powerful front-end framework for faster and easier web development.

Enable | Enable and set default

Figure 4-4. *Enabling the Bootstrap lite theme*

Summary

The module and theme installation process is similar to Drupal 7 with minor differences associated with where you go to find and download a module or theme. In the next chapter, I'll discuss the differences between Backdrop and Drupal 7 modules, and I'll demonstrate how to migrate a custom module from Drupal 7 to Backdrop, including the use of the new configuration management feature in Backdrop.

■ ■ ■

## CHAPTER 5

Converting Modules to Backdrop

One of the advantages that Drupal has over Backdrop is the sheer number of modules that the community has contributed over the years. Backdrop, being the new CMS on the block, lacks the history that Drupal does, but with the underpinning DNA being nearly identical between Backdrop and Drupal 7, the path toward replicating the functional footprint that Drupal contributed modules provide is not too terribly steep.

In this chapter, I'll show how to take an existing Drupal 7 module and modify it so that it works in Backdrop.

Converting the Honeypot Module

The process of migrating a Drupal 7 module to Backdrop is similar to migrating a Drupal module from one major version to another. In the case of migrating a Drupal 7 module to Backdrop, the primary changes are renaming APIs and revising how configuration variables are stored. Backdrop adopted the Drupal 8 concept of storing configuration variables outside of the database. To demonstrate the process, I've selected the Honeypot module, a highly used module in Drupal that is not yet available in Backdrop.

As a courtesy to the module developer, create an issue in the issue queue for the module you want to port, letting the module maintainer know of your intentions. Tag your issue with "backdrop-port" so that others who are considering porting the same module will know that you're already working on it. Figure 5-1 shows the issue I created for the Honeypot module.

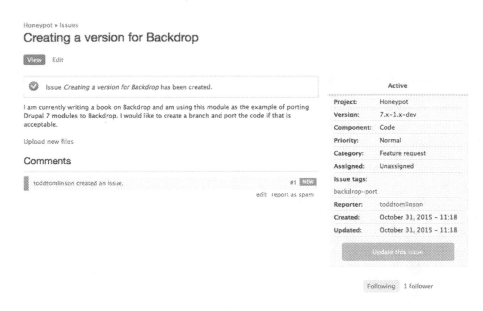

Figure 5-1. *Creating a Backdrop port issue in the issue queue*

Cloning the Drupal 7 Version of the Module

The first step in the process is to clone the Drupal 7 version of the module. Visit the module's page on Drupal.org and click the "Version control" link. Select the highest Drupal 7 version available in the list and click the Show button. In the One-Time Only section of the page, copy the link highlighted in the "Setting up" repository for the first time. In a terminal window, navigate to the root directory of your Backdrop site. In the root directory, navigate to the Modules directory and paste the git clone command copied from the Drupal web site. You should see something similar to the following:

```
git clone --branch 7.x-1.x http://git.drupal.org/project/honeypot.git
Cloning into 'honeypot'...
remote: Counting objects: 802, done.
remote: Compressing objects: 100% (741/741), done.
remote: Total 802 (delta 461), reused 0 (delta 0)
Receiving objects: 100% (802/802), 122.31 KiB, done.
Resolving deltas: 100% (461/461), done.
```

After the clone completes, navigate to the module's directory. In the module's root directory, check to see what branch you are on by entering git branch at the command prompt in your terminal window. The result should be something similar to this:

```
git branch
* 7.x-1.x
```

where 7.x-1.x is the current Drupal 7 branch. The next step is to create a Backdrop-specific branch. To do so, enter the following:

```
git checkout -b 1.x-1.x-for-backdrop
```

Executing the command should result in a message stating that you have been switched to the newly created branch.

```
Switched to a new branch '1.x-1.x-for-backdrop'
```

You are now ready to begin development. As a courtesy, do not commit the branch back to Drupal.org until you have approval from the module maintainer.

Updating the Module's .info File

The first step in modifying the module is to update the .info file. Navigate to the module's root directory using your favorite development tool and change the following elements:

- Change core = 7.x to backdrop = 1.x.

- Any .inc files that are included will need to be removed and replaced with a static class map. Any classes loaded through a .inc file will need to loaded using hook_autoload_info() in the .module file because Backdrop has done away with the class registry.

Next save the module and look to see whether it appears in the list of modules by visiting the /admin/modules page. In the case of the Honeypot module, just by changing core = 7.x to backdrop = 1.x, the module successfully appears in the list of available modules. I'll enable the module and see what breaks.

After enabling the module, I was able to verify that all the normal functionality associated with the Honeypot module works in Backdrop, without any changes other than updating core = 7.x to backdrop = 1.x. Figure 5-2 demonstrates that the Honeypot configuration pages still work the same way they did in Drupal 7.

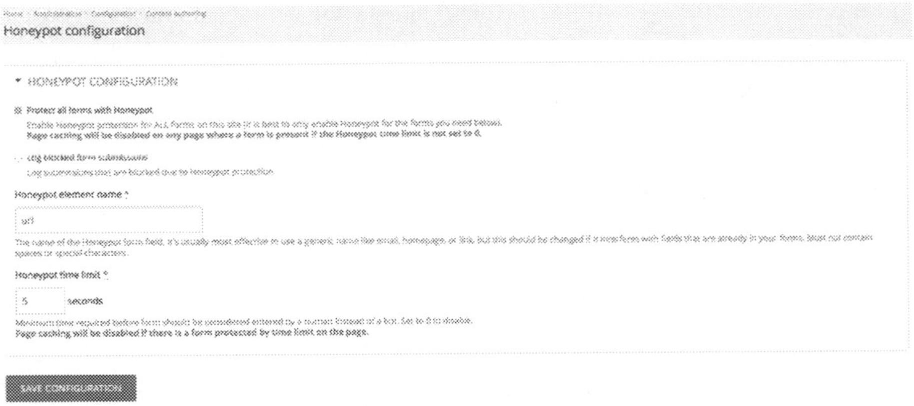

Figure 5-2. *The Honeypot configuration interface on Backdrop*

The module isn't truly ported to Backdrop because it is running in Drupal compatibility mode, a feature that supports the principle of "keep change to a minimum." To port the module, I'll change several other aspects, including renaming APIs, renaming functions, and changing how the configuration management values are stored and retrieved. If you were unable to enable the module, examine the errors that are being displayed, and continue with the process as described next because several of the Drupal APIs have been deprecated in favor of new APIs.

Organizing the Module's Files

The Backdrop team has defined a recommended standard directory structure and file placement within that structure, making it easier for developers and site administrators to find the files they are looking for. The basic recommendations are that all JavaScript files are kept in a `js` folder, CSS files are stored in a `css` folder, templates are stored in a `templates` folder, tests are stored in the `tests` folder, and initial configuration information is stored in the `config` directory. I'll cover configuration management later in this chapter.

The Backdrop team also recommends that the following files be stored in the module's root folder:

- `modulename.info`
- `modulename.module`
- `modulename.admin.inc`
- `modulename.api.php`
- `modulename.pages.inc`
- `modulename.theme.inc`

Renaming the APIs and Functions

The next step is to rename every occurrence of the words *drupal* and *Drupal* with *backdrop* and *Backdrop*. It's critical to turn on case sensitivity when you are globally searching and replacing because *Drupal* has a different meaning than *drupal*, and it's hard to go back and find the right instances to change if you forget to search and replace with case sensitivity turned on.

After searching through all the files associated with the Honeypot module and replacing *Drupal* or *drupal* with *Backdrop* or *backdrop*, I tested the module, and no errors were returned; however, you may not be so lucky. If you encounter errors, the first place to look for information is http://api.backdropcms.org/change-records. This page lists all the changes made while converting Drupal to Backdrop. It's likely that your issue will be well documented in the information contained within this page and its linked resources.

Configuration Management in Backdrop

One of the biggest changes that the Backdrop team made was to externalize configuration variables from the database. Configuration information can now be managed via git and distributed across installations, making it significantly easier to move from a development environment to test and from test to production. While Drupal 8 provides the same functional and technical solution for configuration management, the implementation of the capabilities varies slightly, such as storing the values in JSON instead of YAML, and yes, JSON is a subset of YAML for those of you who are wondering.

Backdrop stores configuration values in files that can be found in the /files/config_xxxxx/active directory. The xxxxxx represents a long string of characters that is created at installation time and defined in settings.php. In the case of my own installation, that directory is named config_408e2eab1311f2c4a572d0a554 eff4c9; however, yours will differ as the string is a unique string by installation. If you navigate to your own config directory, you'll find two subdirectories, active and staging. Navigate to the active directory and view the list of files contained within that directory. You should see a lengthy list of files. Examining one of the configuration files, in this case the admin bar configuration file, you'll see the values that are found in the file and used by the module.

```
{
    "_config_name": "admin_bar.settings",
    "margin_top": 1,
    "position_fixed": 0,
    "components": [
        "admin_bar.icon",
        "admin_bar.menu",
        "admin_bar.search",
        "admin_bar.users",
        "admin_bar.account"
    ]
}
```

The structure of the file is standard JSON notation. For more information on JSON, visit http://json.org.

If your module has a set of predefined variables that are set on installation, you may create a settings file and prepopulate those values in a local settings file in your module's directory. If you have not done so, create a new directory in your module's root directory named config. In that directory, create a new file with a name of xxxxxx.settings.json, where xxxxxx is the name of your module. Following the previous example for the admin_bar module, you may create variables and assign values that will be copied to the active configuration directory in your files/config_xxxxxxxx directory upon installation of your module.

Configuration Management APIs

Drupal made it easy to store configuration information in the database through a set of APIs, specifically, variable_set() and variable_get. Backdrop makes it just as simple by providing a matching set of APIs: config_set() and config_get().

The Backdrop APIs for getting and setting variables differ slightly from the Drupal APIs in that you have the ability to segregate a module's configuration information into separate files based on some criteria that you as the module developer define. A large module with a large number of configuration values might be best served by multiple configuration files with variables grouped in some logical fashion. In other cases, you may decide to store everything in a single file. The decision is up to the module developer and what makes the most sense for your use case. In the case of the Honeypot module, there are a fair number of variables, but they are all interrelated, so I've made the decision to store them in a single file.

The Backdrop API structure for getting, setting, and deleting variables is as follows:

```php
<?php
    config_set('modulename.settings', 'variablename', $value);
?>
```

where modulename is the name of your module. In the case of the Honeypot module, the module name is honeypot. The variablename represents the name of the variable that will be associated with the $value. In cases where you want to segregate variables, you may replace modulename.settings with modulename.subset.settings where subset is a name that you want to use to represent the logical grouping of values. For example, mymodule.urls.settings is a value I would use if I wanted to segregate all variables related to URLs used by a module named mymodule.

```php
<?php
    $variable = config_get('modulename.settings', 'variablename');
?>
```

Similar to the config_set, the config_get takes two parameters: the same modulename.settings value and the name of the variable.

In scenarios where you have a large number of variables that you want to get or set values, Backdrop provides the ability to retrieve all a module's variables as an object and from that object get or set individual values. Here's an example:

```php
<?php
  $config = config('modulename'.settings);
?>
```

The $config object holds all the variables and their values, for example, to retrieve a value from a variable.

```php
$my_variable = $config->get('variablename');
```

The following sets the value of a variable:

```php
$config->set('modulename.settings','variablename', $my_variable);
```

Both functions operate like the config_get and config_set functions but provide a streamlined approach when getting or setting large numbers of variables.

Changing the Module's Admin Interface

Most Drupal modules that use configuration variables provide an admin form as a means for setting and changing the values of the configuration variables. Backdrop provides the same functionality albeit in a slightly different approach. There are three basic changes that I'll have to make to implement configuration management.

1. Change all instances of variable_get() and variable_set() to their Backdrop equivalents.

2. Create a form submit handler and insert a submit button on the admin form.

3. Add a hook_config_info() function to register the configuration variables with the Backdrop configuration system.

I'll start by updating all the instances where existing configuration values are loaded into default form field values. Since there are several values, I'll create a configuration object with all the options and their associated values, minimizing the processing time required to load the form. Technically I could use the config_get() API; however, each call to that API results in the creation of a config object, a call to $config->get() for that option, and the destruction of that object.

At the top of the honeypot_admin_form() function, I'll add the following to create the configuration object:

```php
/* create a configuration object to retrieve existing values from */
  $config = config('honeypot.settings');
```

The next step is to change every instance of `variable_get()` to `$config->get()`. Looking in the `honeypot.admin.inc` file, this is the first instance of a `variable_get` that I found:

```
'#default_value' => variable_get('honeypot_protect_all_forms', 0),
```

I'll change the call from `variable_get` to `$config->get()` as follows:

```
'#default_value' =>
$config->get('honeypot_protect_all_forms'),
```

Note that the option of passing a default value to the function as shown in the previous `variable_get` example has been deprecated in Backdrop because the default values are created and loaded at installation, as described later in this chapter.

I will continue down the list of form fields, replacing every instance of `variable_get()` with the appropriate `$config->get('configuration option')` equivalent.

After changing the `variable_get()` calls, I'll add a submit handler to the admin form because Drupal's `system_settings_form()` API is depreciated in Backdrop. Adding a submit handler is relatively simple; first I'll remove the return `system_settings_form($form);` statement and replace it with the following:

```
$form['actions']['#type'] = 'actions';
  $form['actions']['submit'] = array(
    '#type' => 'submit',
    '#value' => t('Save configuration'),
  );

return $form;
```

I now have a Backdrop-compliant submit button but without `system_settings_form()`. I'll need to write my own form submit handler to save all the configuration values entered on the form.

Creating the Submit Handler

Most modules use the Drupal administration form functionality that includes the `system_settings_form()` function to process and save the values entered on the form. The Honeypot module is somewhat unique in that the module maintainer has written a custom submit handler to perform options outside the scope of the standard functionality provided in the `system_settings_form()` API. A quick search through the `honeypot.admin.inc` file yields a `honeypot_admin_form_submit()` function, so I don't have to create a new function from scratch. Your module may not include an `admin_form_submit` function, and in most cases they won't. In the case where one does not exist, simply add a new function as follows:

```
function modulename_admin_form_submit($form, &$form_state) {
}
```

replacing modulename with the name of your module.

To quickly test to ensure that your admin form is connected to the submit handler, use drupal_set_message() in your admin form submit function.

```
backdrop_set_message("The modules configuration options were successfully
saved");
```

After you've created the message, save your code and test. Pull up the admin form for your module and press the SAVE CONFIGURATION button. You should see your message in the message area of the form, as shown in Figure 5-3.

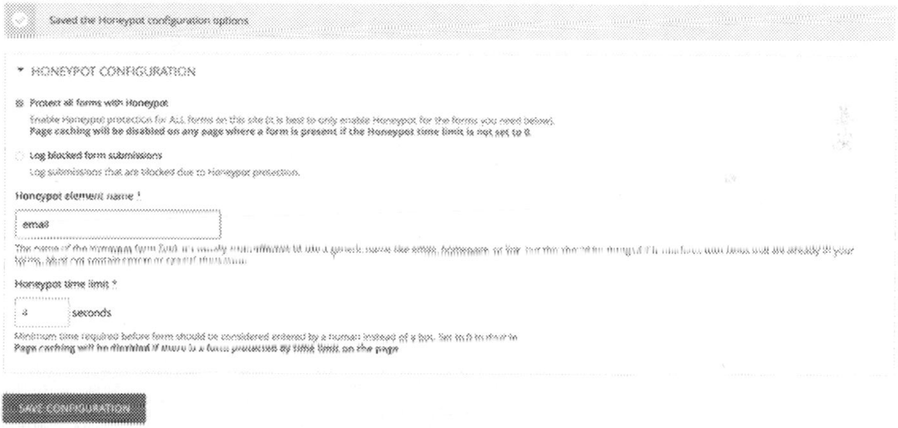

Figure 5-3. *Demonstrating that the submit handler is working*

Next I'll add code to save all the options that a user might enter on the form in the honeypot configuration file. There are two approaches; you can use the config_set('configuration_file_name', 'variable_name', 'value') API, or you can create a configuration object and set each value using the $config->set approach. I'll use the $config->set approach since I have several values to save and the overhead of creating a configuration object for every config_set().

First I'll create a configuration object to hold the values from the form that I need to save by calling the config API, passing it the name of the configuration file that I want to use for this module, honeypot.settings.

```
/* create a configuration object to hold the values */
  $config = config('honeypot.settings');
```

31

Next I'll assign all the values from the $form_state array that is passed into the form's submit handler function to an array named $values. This is an optional step; you may use $form_state['values']['variable_name'] to access the values. Assigning $form_state['values'] to $values shortens the amount of typing I have to do.

```
/* get the values from the submitted form */
  $values = $form_state['values'];
```

I'll then assign each value from the form to a configuration option. You may want to use your favorite debugging technique for listing all the values on the form. I used the Devel module and dpm($form_state['values']) to list all the variables on the form, as shown in Figure 5-4.

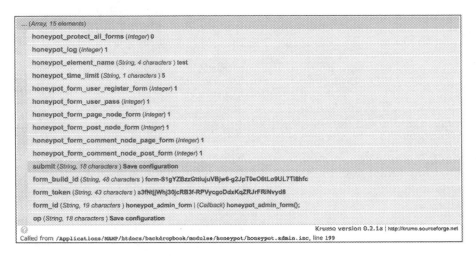

Figure 5-4. *The values from the Honeypot configuration form*

Using the $config object created in the previous step, I'll now use $config->set to store each of the form values into a configuration option.

```
/* assign values from the form to the configuration options */
  $config->set('honeypot_protect_all_forms', $values['honeypot_protect_all_
  forms']);
  $config->set('honeypot_log', $values['honeypot_log']);
  $config->set('honeypot_element_name', $values['honeypot_element_name']);
  $config->set('honeypot_time_limit', $values['honeypot_time_limit']);
  $config->set('honeypot_form_user_register_form', $values['honeypot_form_
  user_register_form']);
  $config->set('honeypot_form_user_pass', $values['honeypot_form_user_pass']);
  $config->set('honeypot_form_page_node_form', $values['honeypot_form_page_
  node_form']);
  $config->set('honeypot_form_post_node_form', $values['honeypot_form_post_
  node_form']);
  $config->set('honeypot_form_comment_node_page_form', $values['honeypot_
  form_comment_node_page_form']);
  $config->set('honeypot_form_comment_node_post_form', $values['honeypot_
  form_comment_node_post_form']);
```

After assigning all the values, the final step is to save the configuration object, which places each of the values into the JSON file, honeypot.settings.json.

```
/* save the configuration options */
  $config->save();
```

After making all the changes to the Honeypot module's configuration form, I'm ready to test. I'll visit admin/config/content/honeypot and enter the values on the form. I'll click the SAVE SETTINGS button, and my expectation is that all the values that I entered will appear on the form after the submit handler executes. After submitting the form with values, they all appear as expected (see Figure 5-5).

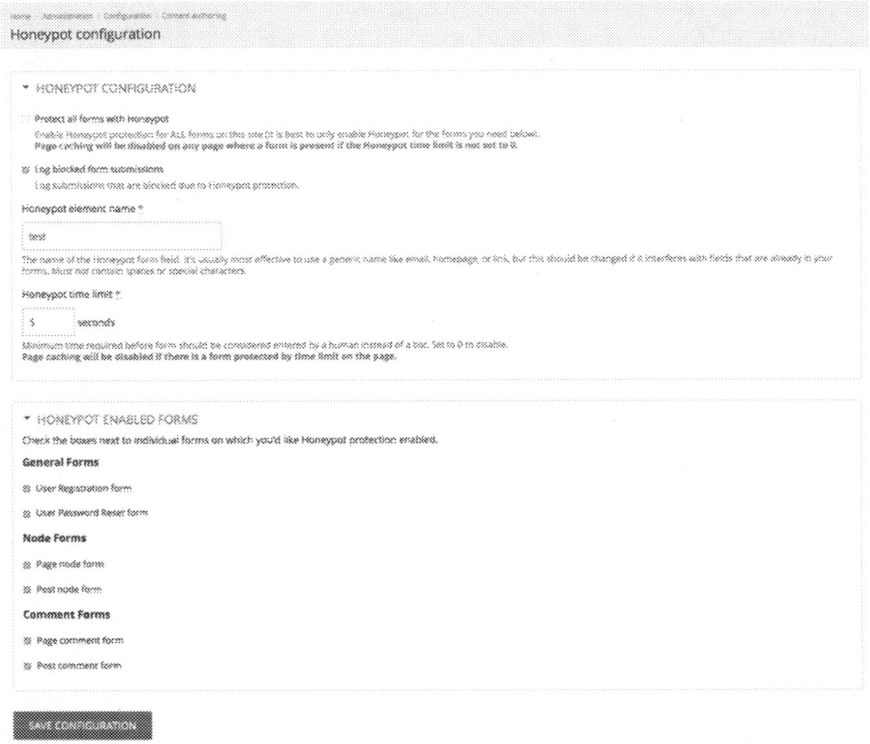

Figure 5-5. *The Honeypot admin form with stored values*

After saving the values and seeing them on the form, I'll visit the `files` directory and look for the `honeypot.settings.json` file in the `config_xxxxxxx/active` directory (where xxxxxxx is your site's specific configuration directory that is created during the installation process). In the directory, I see the `honeypot.settings.json` file, and when examining it, I see all the values that I saved in the admin form submit handler.

```
{
    "_config_name": "honeypot.settings",
    "honeypot_protect_all_forms": 0,
    "honeypot_log": 1,
    "honeypot_element_name": "test",
    "honeypot_time_limit": "5",
    "honeypot_form_user_register_form": 1,
    "honeypot_form_user_pass": 1,
    "honeypot_form_page_node_form": 1,
    "honeypot_form_post_node_form": 1,
    "honeypot_form_comment_node_page_form": 1,
    "honeypot_form_comment_node_post_form": 1,
    "honeypot_log": 1
}
```

Creating a Default Settings File

Some modules have default settings that are set by default when you install the module. To create a default settings file, simply update the module's admin form as you did earlier and enter the default values that you want to include with the base installation of your module. Next, create a `config` directory in your module's root directory and copy the `xxxxxxx.settings.json` file (where xxxxxxx is the name of the settings file you created) from the `files/config_xxxxxx/active` directory into that directory. When your module is enabled for the first time, Backdrop will copy that file into the `files/config_xxxxxx/active` directory.

Registering the Configuration Options

After making the changes, you need to register the configuration options with Backdrop's configuration management processes so the options can be exported. Navigate to `config/development/configuration` and click the single import/export tab. Clicking the Export link near the top right of the page and selecting configuration options from the configuration group field, you'll see that the options for Honeypot are not listed in the drop down (see Figure 5-6).

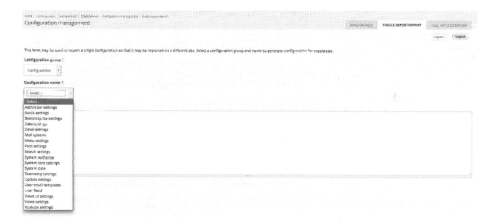

Figure 5-6. *Exporting configuration options*

To add the options so that they are exportable, you need to add a hook_config_
info() call in your module. By visiting http://api.backdropcms.org and searching for
hook_config_info, you'll find a description of the hook as well as sample code. I'll copy
the sample code and modify it slightly for the Honeypot module. In the prefixes array,
I'll add the name of the Honeypot configuration file as the index to the array, and I'll
change the label to Honeypot Settings.

```
/**
 * Implements hook_config_info().
 */
function honeypot_config_info() {

  $prefixes['honeypot.settings'] = array(
     'label' => t('Honeypot Settings'),
     'group' => t('Configuration'),
  );

  return $prefixes;

}
```

After making changes, I'll clear cache from the toolbar by clicking the home icon and
selecting "Flush all cache." I'll revisit the admin/config/development/configuration/
single/export page and select the Configuration option from the "Configuration group"
drop-down list. Checking the "Configuration name" drop-down list, I see that Honeypot
Settings is now present in the list of options, as shown in Figure 5-7.

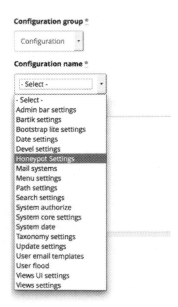

Figure 5-7. *Honeypot Settings in the list of exportable configuration names*

I'll select Honeypot Settings from the list and see that all the options available in the configuration file are present in the interface and selectable for export to other instances of my Backdrop site, such as a testing or production site.

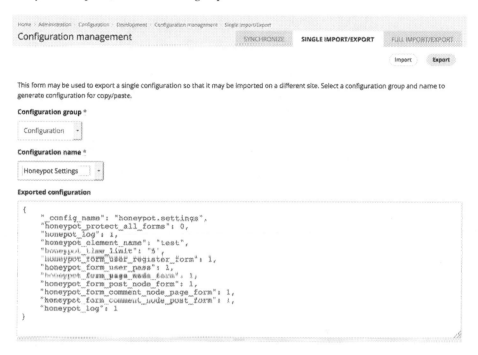

Drupal Compatibility Mode

Backdrop 1.0 includes a Drupal compatibility mode that provides backward compatibility by wrapping all the Drupal APIs in functions that are Backdrop compatible. Compatibility mode is enabled by default in Backdrop 1.0 but may not be present in Backdrop 2.0.

To test your module to see whether it is 100 percent Backdrop and not using the Drupal compatibility mode, edit your settings.php file, found in the root of your Backdrop site, and search for backdrop_drupal_compatibility. You will find a block of code as follows. Change TRUE to FALSE, and you're ready to test your module.

```
/**
 * Drupal backwards compatibility.
 *
 * By default, Backdrop 1.0 includes a compatibility layer to keep it
compatible
 * with Drupal 7 APIs. Backdrop core itself does not use this compatibility
 * layer however. You may disable it if all the modules you're running were
 * built for Backdrop.
 */
$settings['backdrop_drupal_compatibility'] = TRUE;
```

After setting the value to FALSE, I verified that the Honeypot module as updated does not contain any Drupal remnants and is 100 percent Backdrop.

Contributing Your Module to Backdrop

After porting your module to Backdrop, it's a great idea to contribute it to the Backdrop community. Backdrop's success is contingent on the community's contributions to the project. Please participate by contributing your work so that others may leverage the work that you've done. You can find details on how to commit your code in Appendix A.

Summary

In this chapter, I demonstrated porting a Drupal 7 module to Backdrop and the changes that must be made to make a Drupal 7 module 100 percent Backdrop. The process is relatively straightforward, and with a few minor changes, you can port any Drupal 7 module to Backdrop, including implementing Backdrop's configuration management approach.

In the next chapter, I'll cover porting a Drupal 7 theme to Backdrop, which is a significantly easier task than porting modules.

CHAPTER 6

■ ■ ■

Porting Drupal Themes

One of the major changes in Backdrop is the shift in how page layouts are created and managed. In Drupal, the typical solution for creating and managing page layouts is through template files in the theme. Backdrop provides the ability to create and manage page layouts through the Layout module, removing the necessity to create template files for every layout you want to enable in your theme. I'll cover the details of using the Layout module in Chapter 7. There are other minor changes, and I'll cover the details in this chapter as I walk you through the process of porting the Drupal 7 Bluemarine theme (http://drupal.org/project/bluemarine) to Backdrop.

Downloading the Drupal Theme

I will follow the same initial steps that I took to port the Honeypot module, including submitting an issue to the theme's issue queue stating that I intend to port the theme to Backdrop. Themes in Backdrop are stored in the themes directory. You can find the themes directory in the root directory of your Backdrop site. I'll clone the theme into my site's themes directory using the Git clone information found on the theme's version control page. Remember to select the latest Drupal 7 version of the theme. Once the clone has completed, I'll create a new Backdrop branch using git checkout -b '1.x-1.x-backdrop'. I'm now ready to start the process of porting the theme.

The process for porting focuses on changing information in the .info file, changing information in other template files used by the theme, and updating other files such as template.php, replacing anything that contains the words *drupal* with *backdrop* or *Drupal* with *Backdrop*.

Converting the .info File

The primary changes to a theme's .info file are changing core = 7.x to backdrop = 1.x and removing any information relating to regions because layouts are now handled by the Layout module. The following are the changes specific to the Bluemarine theme's .info file:

- Changing core = 7.x to backdrop = 1.x.
- Removing all the regions[xxxxxx] statements.

- Adding a `type = theme` statement to ensure the theme is properly packaged should you decide to contribute it to the Backdrop community.

- Removing global theme settings that are no longer managed by the theme layer. Logo, site name, and site slogan are now set in the Site Information administration page rather than in the theme. You can still use these elements by enabling the Header block in Layouts.

- Removing menus ("Primary links" and "Secondary links"). These are now part of the Layout module and can be enabled by adding the Primary Navigation block.

If your theme contains other statements in the `.info` file, check `http://backdropcms.org/themes` for details on how to support similar functionality in Backdrop.

Converting Other Theme Files

Several changes in the theme layer require modifications to the various `.tpl.php` files, the `template.php` file, and other files contained within a Drupal theme. Many of the changes are because of the removal of Drupal's template process layer and its associated `process_hook()` functions such as `template_process_hook()`, `module_process_hook()`, and `theme_process_hook()`. Any instance of those hooks in your theme will need to be converted to preprocess functions.

Several common elements used in Drupal themes were renamed in Backdrop's theming layer.

- `$classes_array` was renamed to `$classes`.

- `$attributes_array` was renamed to `$attributes`.

- `$title_attributes_array` was removed.

- `$content_attributes_array` was renamed to `$content_attributes`.

- `$html_attributes_array` was renamed to `$html_attributes`.

- `$body_attributes_array` was renamed to `$body_attributes`.

- `$item_attributes_array` was renamed to `$item_attributes`.

Any instance of those arrays will need to be changed when migrating a theme to Backdrop.

There are several changes to common variables that were used in Drupal themes, shifting from referencing variables like $head by calling a function that returns the equivalent renderable elements. Specific changes include the following:

- `print $head;` was changed to `backdrop_get_html_head();`.

- `print $styles;` was changed to `backdrop_get_css();`.

- print $scripts; was changed to backdrop_get_js();.

- print backdrop_get_js('footer') did not exist in Drupal but is a key addition in Backdrop to facilitate moving certain JavaScript files to the end of the page load process.

Other changes to variables include the need to flatten the arrays that were previously translated to strings in Drupal templates.

- Change <?php print $classes; ?> to <?php print implode(' ', $classes); ?>.

- Change <?php print $attributes; ?> to <?php print backdrop_attributes($attributes); ?>.

- Change <?php print $content_attributes; ?> to <?php print backdrop_attributes($content_attributes); ?>.

- Remove any references to $title_attributes because they have been removed.

Comments have also changed in Backdrop and require changes to theme templates. In Drupal comments are stored in $content['comments'], whereas in Backdrop comments are stored in $comments['comments']. The comments form has also changed to $comments['comment_form'].

Several other process hooks were removed from the theming layer in Backdrop and will need to be addressed through other means, specifically:

- contextual_process from modules/contextual/contextual.module

- template_process_layout from modules/layout/includes/layout.theme.inc

- template_process_username from modules/user/user.module

- template_process_views_view from modules/views/theme/theme.inc

Finally, every instance of *drupal* needs to be replaced with *backdrop*, and *Drupal* with *Backdrop*. For example, drupal_add_js() should be backdrop_add_js().

For more information on what has changed, visit http://api.backdropcms.org/developing-themes.

Now that you have this information in hand, I'll walk you through the process of converting the Mayo theme.

Removing page.tpl.php

Page layouts are typically controlled in Drupal's page.tpl.php and its various alternatives for content type–specific layouts, such as page--article.tpl.php (note the two dashes). Backdrop deviates from managing layouts in tpl.php files with the advent of the Layout module, removing the need for a theme-specific page.tpl.php file. There may be CSS class information associated with the elements contained within page.tpl.php that you will want to reuse when you implement layouts. Every theme is different, so it will take a little investigation on your part to identify CSS elements that are unique to your theme's page.tpl.php file. Typically any CSS attribute of #page should be changed to .layout, but it will require analysis on your part to see whether the page-level elements and attributes need to be ported in your CSS files.

Examining Bluemarine's page.tpl.php file, I was unable to identify any CSS elements prefixed with page that I'll want to migrate to the Backdrop version of the theme.

Modifying node.tpl.php

There are a few minor changes to the Mayo theme's node.tpl.php file, specifically addressing flattening the classes and attribute variables used in this template file. The changes that I'll make are as follows:

- Changing `<?php print $classes; ?>` to `<?php print explode(' ', $classes); ?>`

- Changing `<?php print $attributes; ?>` to `<?php print backdrop_attributes($attributes); ?>`

- Removing the reference to $title_attributes

- Changing `<?php print $content_attributes; ?>` to `<?php print backdrop_attributes($content_attributes); ?>`

- Changing `hide($content['comments']);` to `hide($comments['comments']);`

- Changing `<?php print render($content['comments']); ?>` to `<?php print render($comments['comments']); ?>`

- Adding `<?php print render($comments['comment_form']); ?>` immediately following `<?php print render($comments['comments']); ?>`

The next step is to examine the block.tpl.php file and make similar changes. I'll check /core/modules/layout/templates/block.tpl.php for the proper structure for block template files and note that several changes are present in how Backdrop renders blocks.

- `$block->subject` is now just `$title`.

- `$block->body` is now just `$content`.

- `$content_attributes` is no longer needed.

- `print $content` is now `print render($content)`.

- Change `<?php print $classes; ?>` to `<?php print implode(' ', $classes); ?>`.

- Change `<?php print $attributes; ?>` to `<?php print backdrop_attributes($attributes); ?>`.

- Remove `$title_attributes`.

The final step before enabling the theme is to examine the remaining files, such as `template.php`, looking for instances of *drupal* or *Drupal* and replacing them with their Backdrop equivalents of *backdrop* or *Backdrop*.

- For Bluemarine, examining `template.php`, I did not find any instances of *drupal* or *Drupal*. No changes were required.

- In `color.inc`, I found `drupal_add_js()` that I changed to `backdrop_add_js()`.

- In `color/preview.js`, I found `Drupal.color` that I changed to `Backdrop.color` and `Drupal.settings.color.logo` that I changed to `Backdrop.settings.color.logo`.

With all the changes in place, I'm ready to enable the Mayo theme.

Enabling the Ported Theme

As in Drupal, I'll visit the `admin/appearance` page and check to see whether the theme exists in the list of available themes. If it does not appear, check to ensure that you've changed `core = 7.x` to `backdrop = 1.x`. Checking the Disabled Themes section, I see the Bluemarine theme listed (see Figure 6-1).

DISABLED THEMES

Bluemarine

Classic table-based, multi-column, recolorable Backdrop theme.

Enable | Enable and set default

Figure 6-1. *The Bluemarine theme appears in the list of available themes*

I'll click the "Enable and set the default" link. After enabling the Bluemarine theme, I'll visit the home page, and I now see the site rendered using the Mayo theme without any errors, as shown in Figure 6-2.

Figure 6-2. *The Bluemarine theme enabled*

There's more work to do, specifically, creating layouts and assigning blocks that typically were included in the header and footer of a Drupal site into regions in the new layout, which is the focus of the next chapter.

Summary

In this chapter, I covered the basic processes of porting a Drupal theme to Backdrop and the fundamental changes required to make a Drupal theme Backdrop compliant. It's only the start of the process of using the new approach of excluding page layouts and block placement from the theme layer and moving that functionality to Layout, which is the topic of the next chapter.

CHAPTER 7

Creating Layouts

One of the fundamental differences between Backdrop and Drupal is Backdrop's use of the Layout module to create, manage, and control page structure. In Drupal, page structure is typically controlled through template files in the theme or in some cases through the Panels module. In Backdrop, it's all controlled through the Layout module, which is the focus of this chapter.

Default Layouts

The Layout module is included in Backdrop core and is enabled by default during the installation process. To access the Layout administrative user interface, click Structure ➤ Layouts.

During the installation process, the Layout module creates two layouts: a default layout used for all nonadministrative pages on the site and a default administrative layout (see Figure 7-1).

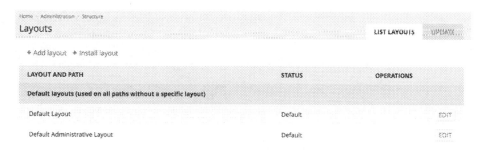

Figure 7-1. The default layouts

There are three basic areas to focus on when looking at layouts.

- What determines when a specific layout is used

- What structure the layout provides, such as one-column, two-column, and so on

- What appears in each area on the page

I'll describe the Default Layout settings to show how the layout is constructed as an example for creating additional layouts. After you click the Edit link associated with the Default Layout section, the module displays a page that shows each of the regions in the layout and the elements that are enabled in each of those regions, as shown in Figure 7-2.

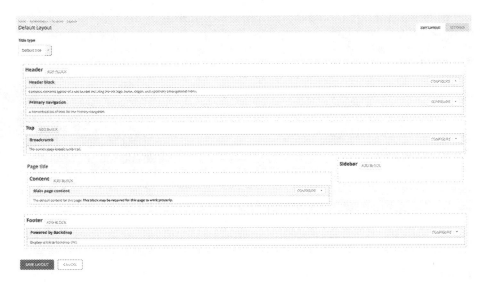

Figure 7-2. *The Default Layout section*

You can see the available layout options by clicking the Settings tab. This page lists the available layouts on your Backdrop site and the layout that is currently assigned, which for me is the two-column layout, as shown in Figure 7-3.

Figure 7-3. *The available layouts*

At this juncture I could add new blocks to the standard layout or change the physical structure of the layout using the pages shown in Figure 7-2 and Figure 7-3. Instead of changing the defaults, I'll proceed by creating a custom layout.

Creating Custom Layouts

In the current state, the default layout is applied to every page of the site. There are likely scenarios where there are requirements for a different physical layout and the elements that appear on the page. I'll demonstrate this by creating a new layout that will be used by the pages on the site that display an individual node.

I'll start the process of creating a new custom layout by clicking the Add Layout link at the top of the Layout administration page, as shown in Figure 7-2. The first form in the process provides the ability to specify a name of the new layout, the structural layout of the page, and the path structure that will determine when this layout will be used (see Figure 7-4).

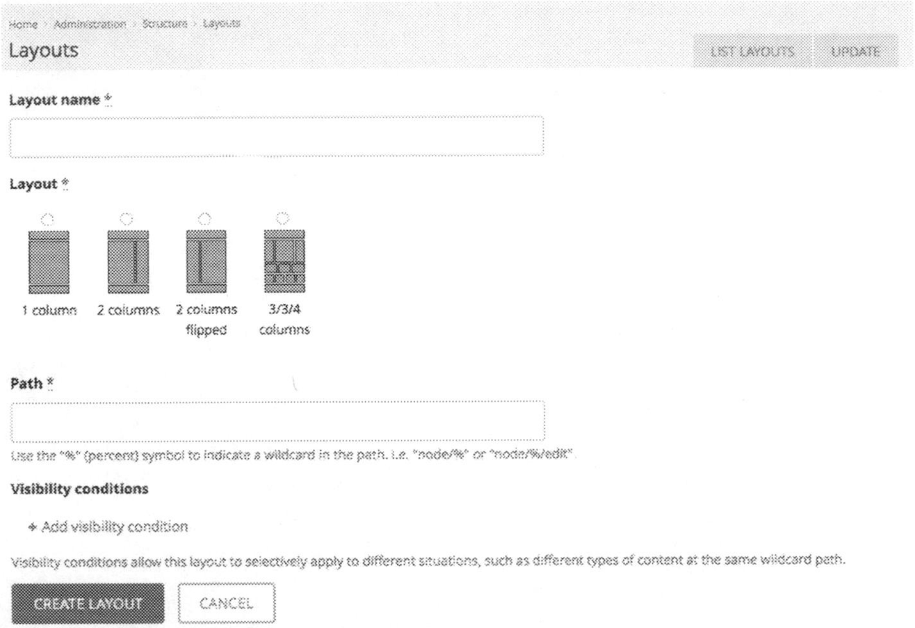

Figure 7-4. *Creating a custom layout*

I'll use *node* as the layout name, the single-column layout, and a path of node/% to control when this template will be used. After entering the path, I now have the ability to specify additional criteria to further refine when this template will be used by clicking the Add Visibility condition button, as shown in Figure 7-5. Clicking the button exposes a list of options, including the ability to specify the node type, whether the page being rendered is the front page of the site, whether a specific language is enabled, whether a user permission or role is set, and additional URL information.

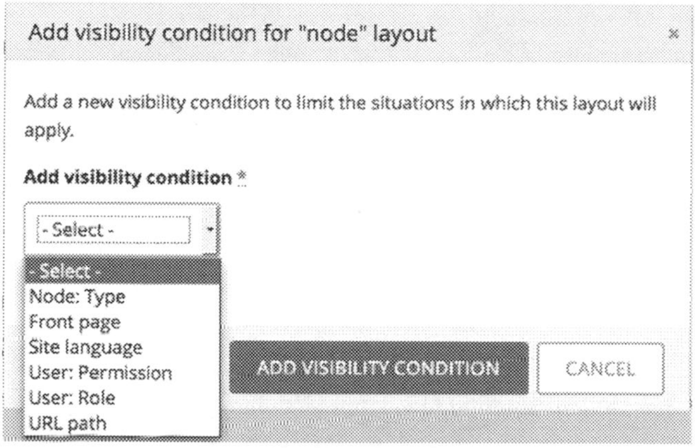

Figure 7-5. *Additional visibility conditions*

After I select Node: Type, the module displays a check list with all the content types enabled on the site, allowing a site builder to define a specific layout by content type. Selecting "Front page" displays a list of two conditions: use the template only if the visitor is on the front page of the site or use this template only if the visitor is not on the front page. In the case of a node-specific template, the only viable option would be not on the front page. Selecting "Site language" results in a list of enabled languages on the site, allowing a site administrator to control when this layout will be used based on activated language. Selecting User: Permission results in a list of all the site's permissions, enabling restriction based on the visitor's enabled permissions. Selecting User: Role performs a similar function of displaying all the roles enabled on the system, allowing restriction based on the visitor's assigned roles. Selecting URL path provides an interface to specify additional URL details, including paths to include and paths to exclude. You may accumulate visibility conditions by selecting and adding one or more of the items described earlier, providing a fine level of granular control over when a specific layout will be applied to a page.

For the node template that I'm creating, I'll keep it simple and not add visibility conditions beyond the path specified in the Path field. I'll click the Create layout button to continue to assigning elements to the regions on the layout, as shown in Figure 7-6.

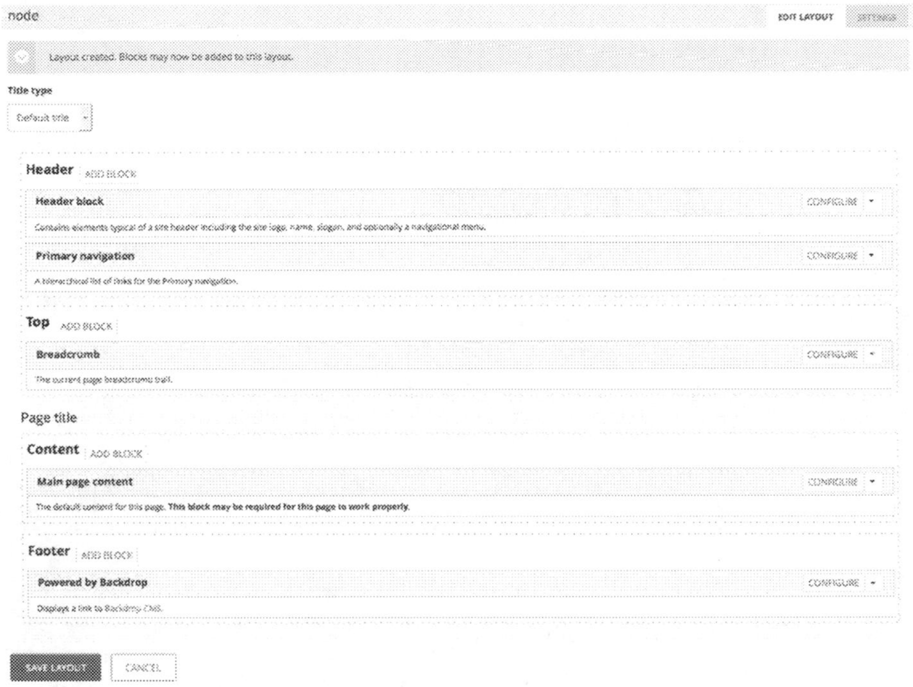

Figure 7-6. *Assigning elements to regions*

When the Layout module creates the new layout, it automatically copies all the elements assigned to regions in the default layout to the new custom layout. At this juncture, I could rearrange the elements by dragging and dropping them on different regions of the layout, I could remove elements from the layout, or I could add new elements that do not appear in the standard layout. To demonstrate the capabilities, I will do the following:

- Remove the Powered by Backdrop block from the footer
- Create a new custom block to insert into the footer

To remove the Powered by Backdrop block, I'll click the arrow next to the Configure link, selecting the Remove option. To create a new custom block, I'll open a new tab in my browser and navigate to Structure ➤ Custom blocks, selecting the "Add block" link to create a new block. The block creation process is similar to Drupal: enter a name, title, and body content, as shown in Figure 7-7.

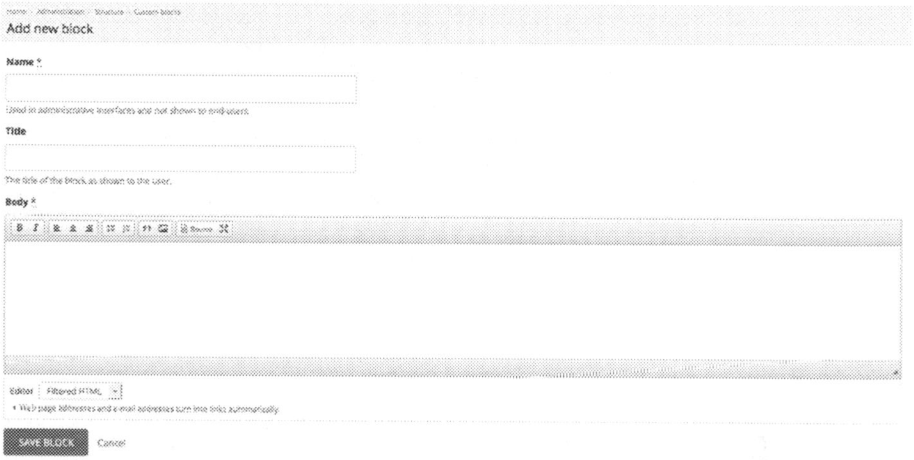

Figure 7-7. *Creating a custom block*

After saving the new block, I'll return to the new layout and add the new custom block to the Footer region by clicking the Add Block button and selecting my new block from the list of available blocks, as shown in Figure 7-8

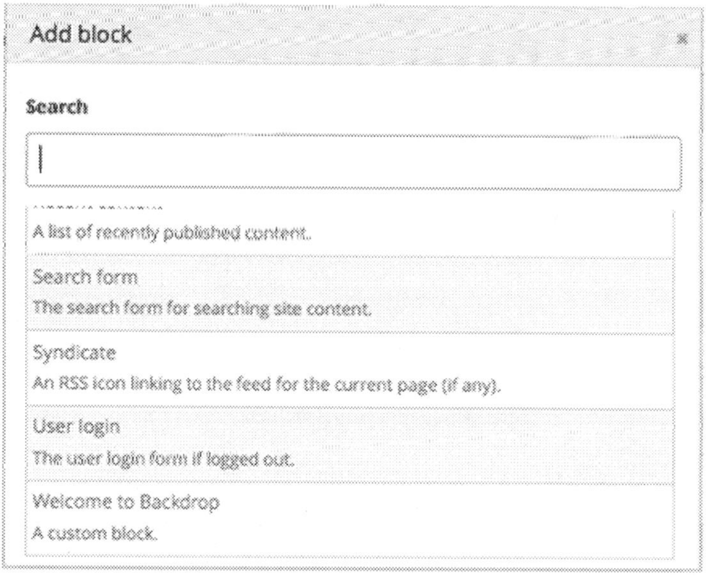

Figure 7-8. *The list of available blocks*

51

Selecting my custom Welcome to Backdrop block, I am then presented with a list of options to configure the block for this specific layout, including modifying the title, body, style settings, and block visibility parameters, similar to Drupal's approach (see Figure 7-9).

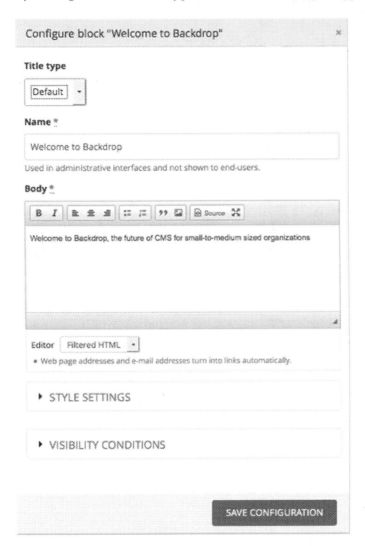

Figure 7-9. Configuring a block for placement on a layout

With the layout complete, I'm now ready to test by creating a new node and viewing that node to validate that the new layout is being used. I'll click the Save Layout button at the bottom of the page, which returns me to the list of available layouts, showing the new layout that I just created as a custom layout (see Figure 7-10).

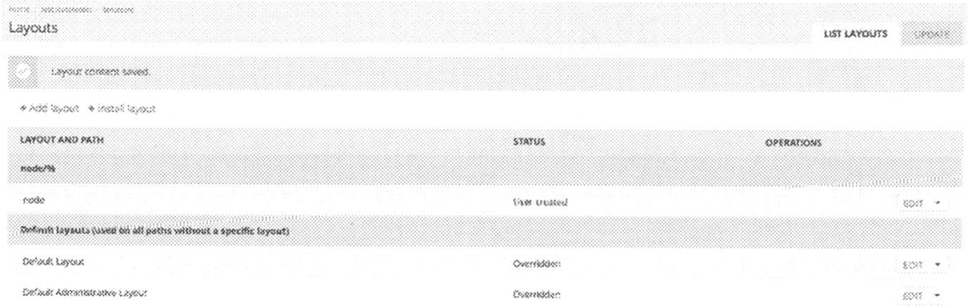

Figure 7-10. *The revised list of available layouts*

After creating a new post content item and viewing the content, I can verify that the new layout is being used to render the page, as shown in Figure 7-11. I can tell the new layout is being used because the footer has the new custom block that I created and does not show the Powered by Backdrop block that appears on the home page of the site.

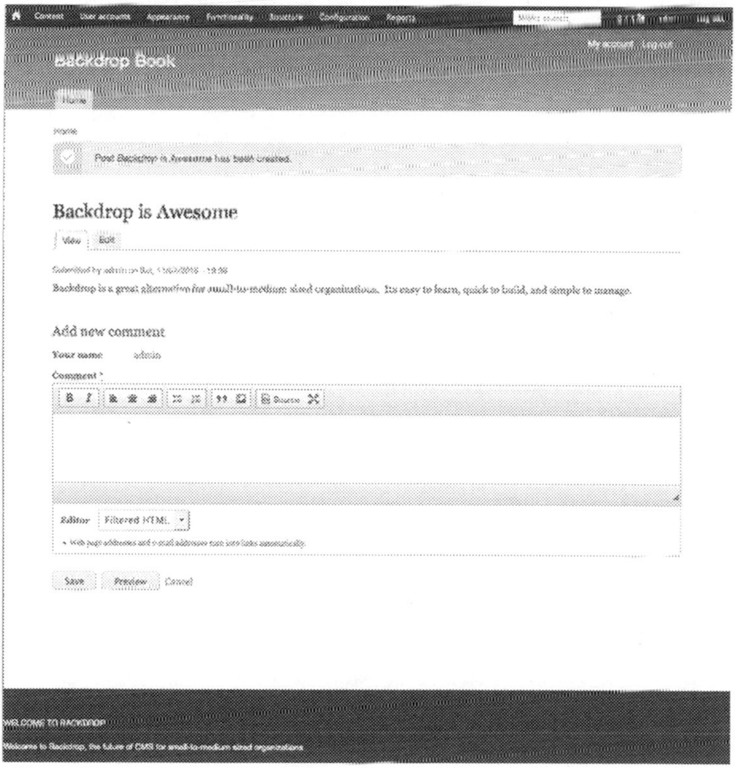

Figure 7-11. *Rendering a node using the new layout*

Installing Other Layouts

While the basic layouts that come with Backdrop core may suffice for your site, there are a growing number of contributed layouts that you can install on your site. You may find the additional layouts by visiting http://backdropcms.org/layouts or on GitHub at http://github.com/backdrop-contrib and then search for Layout. I'm a fan of the Radix layouts and have used them on a majority of my sites over the past year. I'll add those layouts to my Backdrop site to provide several additional structural layouts beyond the four standard structural layouts that come with Backdrop's Layout module.

The Radix layouts are found on Backdrop's GitHub site and can be downloaded or cloned by visiting http://github.com/backdrop-contrib/radix_layouts. I'll use Git to clone the Radix layouts in the site's layouts directory, which can be found in the root directory of the Backdrop site. After cloning into layouts/radix, I now have several additional layouts that I'm ready to enable and use. After cloning the layouts and clearing cache, I can now see all the additional layouts provided by Radix by clicking the "add layout" link on the Layout administration page (see Figure 7-12).

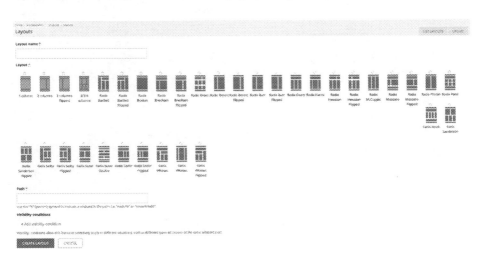

Figure 7-12. *The additional Radix layouts*

Creating a Custom Layout Template

While the combination of the off-the-shelf layouts provided by the Layout module when combined with Radix offers a wide variety of structural layout options, there may be cases where you need a layout that doesn't exist. Creating a layout is relatively straightforward, and if you have created custom panel layouts in Panels in Drupal, you'll recognize the process.

A custom structural layout has four basic elements:

- A directory in the layouts directory named to match the name of the custom layout, for example, my_layout

- An .info file within the layouts directory with the same name as the directory that it resides in, for example, my_layout.info

- A .png file that represents the structure of the physical layout, for example, my_layout.png

- A template file, for example, my_layout.tpl.php

- A stylesheet with the associated CSS for the layout, for example, my_layout.css, stored in a css subdirectory

Creating the Layout's .info File

The content of the .info file is similar to a theme's .info file. Take as an example, the .info file for my_layout. Unlike a theme that doesn't deal with regions, a layout does specify regions because it is the entity responsible for creating and managing the structure of pages. In the case of my_layout, there are three regions: Header, Content, and Footer.

```
name = My Layout
version = BACKDROP_VERSION
backdrop = 1.x

; Specify regions for this layout.
regions[header] = Header
regions[content] = Content
regions[footer] = Footer

; Default region.
default region = ''

; Preview
preview = my_layout.png

; Default stylesheets
stylesheets[all][] = ../css/my_layout.css
```

I'll save the my_layout.info file and continue with the template.

Creating the Layout's .tpl.php File

The `.tpl.php` file looks identical to a theme template file because it is in essence just that—a theme template that is managed by the Layout module. The content of `my_layout.tpl.php` is as shown next. It follows the structural changes to `.tpl.php` files as discussed in Chapter 6 and follows the familiar conventions of a typical Drupal template file.

```php
<?php
/**
 * @file
 * Template for My Layout.
 */
?>
<div class="my-layout <?php print implode(' ', $classes); ?>"<?php print
backdrop_attributes($attributes); ?>>
  <?php if (!empty($content['header'])): ?>
    <header id="header" class="header" role="header">
      <div class="container">
        <?php print $content['header']; ?>
      </div>
    </header>
  <?php endif; ?>

  <?php if ($messages): ?>
    <section class="messages container">
      <?php print $messages; ?>
    </section>
  <?php endif; ?>

  <main class="main container" role="main">
    <div class="page-header">
      <a id="main-content"></a>
      <?php print render($title_prefix); ?>
      <?php if ($title): ?>
        <h1 class="title" id="page-title">
          <?php print $title; ?>
        </h1>
      <?php endif; ?>
      <?php print render($title_suffix); ?>
    </div>

    <?php if ($tabs): ?>
      <div class="tabs">
        <?php print $tabs; ?>
      </div>
    <?php endif; ?>
```

```php
  <?php print $action_links; ?>
  <div class="container-fluid">
    <div class="row">
      <div class="col-md-12 my-layout-layouts-contentmain">
        <?php print $content['content']; ?>
      </div>
    </div>
  </div>
</main>

<?php if ($content['footer']): ?>
  <footer id="footer" class="footer" role="footer">
    <div class="container">
      <?php print $content['footer']; ?>
    </div>
  </footer>
<?php endif; ?>
</div><!-- /.my_layout -->
```

Creating the Layout's .css File

Using standard CSS, I'll create my layout's CSS to address how I want the layout to render and how it behaves through the various breakpoints, making the layout responsive. There are nearly 1,000 lines of CSS for my layout, so to honor brevity, I won't paste the CSS here. However, there is not anything that is unique about a layout's CSS file outside of what you would implement in a typical theme.

After saving all the files and clearing cache, I can now use my custom layout as it appears in the list of available layouts, as shown in Figure 7-13.

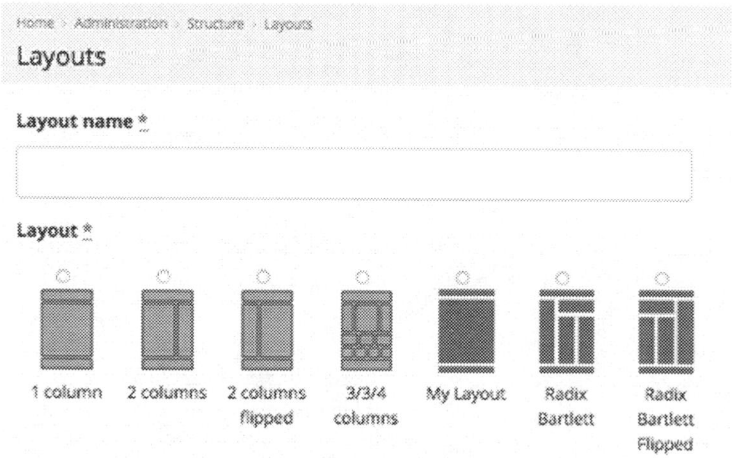

Figure 7-13. My layout available for use

Changing Layouts

Over time you may run into instances where you have a page assigned to a specific layout and you need to change the physical structure of that page. You may do so by navigating to Structure ➤ Layouts and clicking the Edit link for the layout you want to change. On the layout's configuration page, click the Settings tab at the top, select a different layout, and click the Save Layout button. On the Edit layout tab, you may then rearrange the blocks into regions, add new blocks, or remove existing blocks.

Summary

The Layout module provides a simple-to-use interface for managing the structure of the pages rendered on your site. The ability to configure with layouts that are based on fine-grained controls make the module a powerful solution for creating beautifully structured pages across a Backdrop site, with little to no programming required. The Layout module also provides the flexibility to integrate contributed layouts, such as Radix, and the ability to create your own custom layouts.

In the next chapter, I'll walk you step by step through the process of migrating a Drupal 7 site to Backdrop, a scenario that many small to medium-sized organizations may undertake in the near term.

CHAPTER 8

■ ■ ■

Migrating to Backdrop

Backdrop provides a relatively easy migration path for those interested in moving from Drupal 7 to Backdrop. The migration effort is on the same order of magnitude as migrating a Drupal site to the next version of Drupal, with a few minor differences in the availability of equivalent contributed modules. Backdrop is relatively new and does not have the inventory of contributed modules that Drupal does.

In this chapter, I'll walk you step-by-step through the process of migrating a typical Drupal 7 site to Backdrop. Your site may differ based on the number of contributed and custom modules and themes; however, the general process is the same.

Evaluating Your Drupal Site

The first step in the process is to examine your existing Drupal site and determine the best path for migration. The following are the items to examine:

- The Drupal 7 core modules that your site uses to deliver functionality to site visitors and administrators. There are a number of Drupal 7 core modules that were removed in favor of simplifying the platform. The modules include the following:

  - Aggregator

  - Blog

  - Dashboard

  - Forum

  - Help

  - OpenID

  - Overlay

  - PHP filter

  - Poll

  - Profile

- RDF

- Shortcut

- Statistics

- Tracker

- Trigger

- Backdrop also removed core support for databases other than MySQL, MariaDB, or equivalent, such as PostgreSQL. There may be contributed equivalents for some of these modules. The list of contributed modules is continuously growing. Check http:// backdropcms.org/modules for a current list of available modules.

- Contributed modules. One of the benefits of Drupal is the large number of contributed modules that are available to extend the functionality of your site. Backdrop, being a relatively new CMS platform, lacks the sheer volume of available contributed modules. However, with the steps outlined in Chapter 4, most developers can in a matter of minutes or hours port an existing Drupal 7 contributed module to Backdrop. The next step is to evaluate which contributed modules your site relies on and whether an equivalent exists in Backdrop. If a module has not been ported, the decision rests on whether the functionality is absolutely required, whether there is a functionally equivalent module in Backdrop, whether the functionality can be accomplished through other means that are available in Backdrop, or whether you are willing to port the Drupal 7 module to Backdrop.

- Custom modules. Any custom module that you have developed will need to be ported using the steps outlined in Chapter 5. As with all migrations, now is a good time to assess whether the functionality provided by your custom modules can be replaced with off-the-shelf Backdrop core or contributed modules.

- Theme. If you used a core or contributed theme for your site, look to see whether a Backdrop equivalent exists. If a Backdrop version of a contributed theme does not exist, consider porting the theme as outlined in Chapter 6 and contribute the Backdrop version to the community. If your site uses a custom theme, you will need to port the theme using the steps outlined in Chapter 6. As with custom modules, now is a perfect time to evaluate whether a better solution exists in the list of contributed themes at http://backdropcms.org/themes.

- Layouts. Backdrop's use of the Layout module to create and manage page layouts requires removing any layout structures you have in your template files or modules such as Panels. Inventory the page layouts on your site and determine whether the Layout module's off-the-shelf or contributed layouts fulfill the needs of your site. If there are layouts that cannot be fulfilled with off-the-shelf layouts, determine whether the page structure can be retrofitted into an existing layout or whether you are prepared to create a custom layout, as shown in Chapter 7.

Preparing Your Drupal Site for the Upgrade

With the evaluation complete and the list of changes required to migrate your site to Backdrop, the next step in the process is to prepare your Drupal site for the migration process. There are several recommended activities that will ensure that your migration works as smoothly as possible.

Upgrade Your Drupal 7 Site to the Latest Version

The first step in the process is to ensure that your Drupal 7 site is running the latest version of Drupal 7. You can check the status of your site by visiting admin/reports/updates. If you are running the latest version, you can skip this section and proceed. If you need to update Drupal, follow these steps:

1. Back up your site. Ensure that your backup completed successfully and is complete before proceeding.

2. Log in as a user with the permission "Administer software updates."

3. If you are updating a live, production site, go to Administration ➤ Configuration ➤ Development ➤ Maintenance mode. Enable the "Put site into maintenance mode" check box and save the configuration.

4. Remove all old core files and directories, except for the sites directory, the original install profile in the profiles directory, and any custom files you added elsewhere. In your Drupal root folder, delete all files and the following folders: includes, misc, modules, scripts, and themes. If you used a normal installation, then also delete the profiles folder, but if you used a custom profile, then in the profiles folder, delete the subfolders minimal, standard, and testing.

5. If you made modifications to the file .htaccess or robots.txt, you will need to re-apply them from your backup, after the new files are in place.

6. Update your `settings.php` file. In some instances, an update includes changes to `settings.php` as noted in the new release notes for the new version. If that's the case, replace your old `settings.php` with the new `default.settings.php` file, and copy the site-specific entries (especially the lines giving the database name, user, and password) from the old `settings.php` to the new `settings.php`.

7. If you had added any custom templates or other custom files outside the `sites` folder, then you will need to restore them from your backup because they have been deleted.

8. Download the latest Drupal 7.*x* release from `http://drupal.org/ project/drupal` to a directory outside your web root. Extract the archive and copy the files into your Drupal directory. This will (a) install fresh copies of the files and subfolders deleted in step 3, (b) overwrite any files in the `sites` folder that are part of core (e.g., `sites/all/README.txt` and `sites/default/ default.settings.php`), and (c) leave alone any file in the `sites` folder whose path and name are different from any file in core. As an alternative, you could (a) copy all the files and folders except `sites` from the new core you downloaded into your Drupal root; (b) if the release notes indicate there have been changes to `settings.php`, then replace your `default. settings.php` with the new version in your download, replace your current `settings.php` with a copy of the new `default. settings.php`, and insert any site-specific content from current `settings.php` into the new one; and (c) repeat step (b) for all additional sites in a multisite installation.

9. Re-apply any modifications to files such as `.htaccess` and `robots.txt` and restore any deleted templates or other custom files you had in core folders.

10. Run `update.php` by visiting `/update.php`. This will update the core database tables.

11. In a multisite installation, run `update.php` again for each site.

12. Go to Administration ➤ Reports ➤ Status report. Verify that everything is working as expected.

13. Ensure that `$update_free_access` is `FALSE` in `settings.php`.

14. Go to Administration ➤ Configuration ➤ Development ➤ Maintenance mode. Disable the "Put site into maintenance mode" check box and save the configuration.

15. Back up your site again.

At this point, you should be running the latest version of Drupal 7 and are ready to move to the next step in the process.

Update All Your Contributed Modules to the Latest Version

With Drupal 7 core updated to the latest version, the next step in the process is to update all the contributed modules to their latest stable release. Visit admin/reports/updates and identify modules that need to be updated. If you find modules that are out of date, first evaluate whether the update will cause issues on your site.

- Check the module's documentation to see whether any patches were applied or customizations were made to the module for your specific site. While best practice is to make any changes to a module's functionality through a custom module that utilizes the contributed module's hooks, not all developers follow best practices, and there may be cases where someone has directly modified a module. If no apparent updates were made, you may want to compare the source of the same version of the module you have installed with the original source on Drupal.org for that module. If there were changes to a contributed module's source, you'll need to determine a path to ensure that the updated functionality is replicated in the newest version of that module.

- Read the module's documentation, typically the READ.me file, to see whether there are any constraints or conditions that may affect other modules. For example, an update to CTools may impact views. If there are other modules that are affected, ensure that updating one module will not negatively impact the other related modules.

- Read the release notes for the newest version of the module. Check to see whether the update contains new features or bug fixes that are not critical to your web site. If they are not critical, you may choose to not update the module before porting to Backdrop.

- Check to see whether any of the changes are security related. Evaluate the criticality of the security flaw and determine whether your site is vulnerable. If not, you may choose to skip the update.

- Check the module's issue queue to see whether any new issues have been logged for the latest update. If so, determine whether those issues will impact your site.

If all looks well with the newest version of the module update it using the following steps:

1. Place your site in maintenance mode. Visit admin/config/development/maintenance and select the appropriate options.

2. Back up the site including the database.

63

3. Remove the existing module's files from within its root directory.

4. Download the latest version of the module and uncompress the files in the module's root folder.

5. Check `admin/modules` to ensure that the new version of the module is recognized by your site and is enabled.

6. Check the status of your site by visiting `/admin/reports/status` to see whether `update.php` needs to be run to update the schema of your database. If the report shows a pending database change, run `/update.php`.

7. Test the functionality provided by the new module. If all seems well, back up the site again and take the site out of maintenance mode.

Disable and Uninstall Core Modules That Have Been Removed

As listed in the "Evaluating Your Drupal Site" section earlier in this chapter, several Drupal 7 core modules have been removed from Backdrop. Those modules must be disabled and removed prior to migrating the site to Backdrop. The process for disabling these modules includes the following steps:

1. Visit the `admin/modules` page of your site and using the list of modules provided in the "Evaluating Your Drupal Site" section of this chapter, determine whether any of those modules are enabled on your site and, if enabled, whether they have been used.

2. If you have used modules such as the Blog, Forum, or Poll modules, you'll need to remove all the content associated with the entities created by those modules before disabling and removing the module. You may delete the content or migrate the content to a custom content type. To migrate the content to a new custom content type, consider using the Migrate module or extracting the content using views and importing using feeds.

Install the Token Module

If your Drupal 7 site does not use the Token module, you'll need to install it to successfully run the `update.php` process in Backdrop because Backdrop assumes the tables associated with the Token module already exist. Install Token following the standard procedures for installing a Drupal 7 module and enable it to create the base tables for Token. You may skip this step if your site is already using the Token module.

Change Your Theme

The next step in the process is to change your theme back to a Drupal 7 core theme, including your administrative theme. The process for changing your theme is as follows:

1. Visit the admin/appearance page.

2. Click the "Enable and set default" link for the Bartik theme.

3. Set the administration theme to Seven.

4. Disable your other enabled themes.

5. Click "Save configuration."

Back Up and Prepare for the Migration

The final steps in preparing your Drupal 7 site for the migration are to set the site into maintenance mode if it is not already in that mode (/admin/config/development/maintenance) and to back up the site, including the database and files directory. At this point, you are ready to proceed with the migration to Backdrop.

Migrating Your Site to Backdrop

With all the preparation work complete, you are now ready to perform the migration to Backdrop. I highly recommend trying the upgrade on a copy of your site in a directory outside of your production version of the site. While it is possible to migrate in the existing root directory of your site, the risks significantly outweigh the rewards. Just don't do it.

1. You'll need a clean copy of the configuration parameters for a standard Backdrop installation. Since I am skipping the actual step of running the Backdrop installer, I'll create a temporary installation of Backdrop following the steps outlined in Chapter 2. I'll need all the files in the /files/config_XXXXXXXXX/active directory to successfully bootstrap Backdrop after I walk you through the following steps. Now is a great time to take that step and to have the config files ready to copy.

2. If you decide to accept the risk of migrating your site in the production directory, the first step is to delete everything outside of your /sites/default/files directory. Again, the recommendation is to not attempt this in your existing Drupal installation's directories; proceed with extreme caution. Again, just don't do it; create a new directory.

3. Following the steps outlined in Chapter 2, download a new copy of Backdrop from backdropcms.org and expand the compressed file before proceeding.

4. Create the new MySQL database that will be used to store the last backup copy of your Drupal 7 site.

5. Copy the `files` directory contents from your Drupal 7 site, typically at `/sites/default/files` to your Backdrop files directory in the root directory of your Backdrop site, `/files`.

6. Import your Drupal 7 database backup into the database created for your new Backdrop site using your favorite database import tool, as in `mysql -uusername -ppassword databasename < backupfile.sql`, where `username`, `password`, `databasename`, and `backupfile.sql` are all placeholders for the values that you used to create the database, the database user, and the name of the backup file.

7. Update Backdrop's `settings.php` file with database connection information for the new Backdrop database that you just imported the Drupal 7 backup into. You take this step instead of running the normal installation process as you want to use the values already stored in the database and you are not starting with a new site. The specific statement to update in `settings.php` is `$database = 'mysql://user:pass@localhost/ database_name';`.

8. Replace `user`, `pass`, and `database_name` with the appropriate values.

9. Run `update.php` after setting the database parameters to get the name of the directory where your configuration files will reside. This step is necessary because the name of the configuration directory is based on an MD5 hash of the database object. When executing `update.php`, you'll see an error that states that your configuration directory is missing or empty. Use the name of the directory as stated in the error message to create the configuration directory in the `files` directory. The structure of the name will be `config_xxxxxxxx`, where xxxxxxxx represents the MD5 hash value of your database object. Make sure that the directory you create to house the configuration files is set to the correct permissions so that the web server can create and write those files; typically, `chmod 644` will suffice.

10. Copy all the config settings files in the site that you installed during the first step of this process into the `files/config_ XXXXXXXXXXX/active` directory of your migrated site, replacing the XXXXXXXXXX with the actual values found on your new site.

11. Download contributed modules, themes, and layouts for your new Backdrop site and place them in the appropriate directories, remembering that you haven't copied anything from your Drupal 7 site other than the database and your `files` directory.

12. In a text editor, update the `settings.php` file, changing `$settings['update_free_access'] = FALSE;` to `$settings['update_free_access'] = TRUE;`. This will allow you to run `update.php` without being logged in as a site administrator.

13. Navigate to the site in a browser and visit `update.php` to proceed with the update. You'll likely see 100+ updates that need to be applied to.

14. After running `update.php`, change the value for `update_free_ access` in `settings.php` back to `FALSE` before proceeding.

15. Navigate to the home page of your site and log in using your Drupal 7 credentials. You should see a successfully migrated site, as shown in my ported site in Figure 8-1.

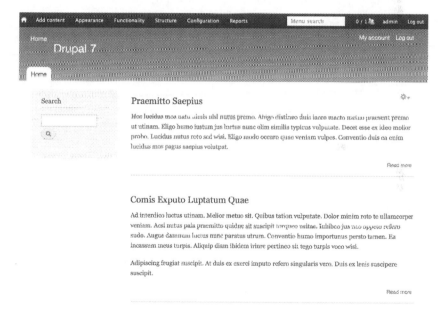

Figure 8-1. *My Drupal 7 site running in Backdrop*

You may encounter other errors as you migrate your Drupal 7 site to Backdrop, and it's difficult to predict all the potential errors that you may encounter because of the flexibility and extensibility of Drupal. If you do run into errors, I suggest searching the http://backdropcms.org site as a first step. These are other tools that you may want to use:

- Checking the issue queue on GitHub at http://github.com/backdrop/backdrop-issues/issues

- Looking through the API documentation at http://api.backdropcms.org/

- Looking through change records at https://api.backdropcms.org/change-records

- Joining the weekly meetings on Thursdays at 1 p.m. Pacific on Google+ at https://plus.google.com/+BackdropcmsOrg

- Checking out the various videos on Backdrop's YouTube channel at https://www.youtube.com/user/backdropcms

- Visiting Backdrop's Reddit community at http://www.reddit.com/r/backdrop/

- Live chat by participating in Backdrop's IRC at irc://irc.freenode.net/backdrop

- Following Backdrop on Twitter at http://twitter.com/backdropcms

- Or visiting the Backdrop Facebook page at www.facebook.com/backdropcms

Next Steps

After migrating your site to Backdrop, the next steps are to bring your site back to its original state by addressing four key areas.

- Check the theme that you used on your Drupal 7 version of your site. If you used a contributed theme, check http://backdropcms.org/themes to see whether a Backdrop version of that theme exists. If not, you could choose to port the theme as outlined in Chapter 6, select a different theme that has already been ported to Backdrop, or create a new Backdrop theme following the guidelines outlined at http://api.backdropcms.org/themes.

- Re-create page layouts. If your Drupal 7 site relied on template files or panels for page layouts, you'll need to re-create those layouts using the Layout module, as described in Chapter 7.

- Validate block positioning. Because of the change in how Backdrop handles layouts, blocks may need to be repositioned on your new site. Follow the examples in Chapter 7 on how to use the Layout module to place blocks in regions.

- Check views. During the migration process, Backdrop will attempt to port your Drupal 7 views, but there are some Drupal 7 views components that do not have comparable equivalents in Backdrop.

- Check contrib projects. All contrib project should contain upgrade paths from Drupal 7 to Backdrop; however, there may be cases where your site's use of a module has not been thoroughly tested.

- Test your site before turning it loose on your visitors. The port to Backdrop is not trivial in nature, so it's critical to test every aspect of your web site before turning visitors loose. After testing, make sure you have a clean backup of your Backdrop site and then move your newly ported site into your production directory.

Porting Other CMSs and Drupal Versions

The only current supported migration path to Backdrop is from Drupal 7. If your site is running Drupal 6 and you want to port to Backdrop, you have two options.

- Port your Drupal 6 site to Drupal 7 and then to Backdrop. See Chapter 9 for a guide on upgrading from Drupal 6 to 7.

- Rebuild your site in Backdrop.

Either option requires significant work. Those running Drupal 6 sites are quickly coming to a crossroads where running on an unsupported platform will require a decision about whether to continue running a production site on an unsupported platform or whether to take the time to migrate to a newer version of Drupal or to Backdrop.

Porting other CMS platforms to Backdrop is equivalent to porting other CMS platforms to Drupal. Currently there are no automated means or guides to perform non-Drupal 7 migrations to Backdrop; however, those familiar with the Migrate module may use the same approaches for migrating a non-Drupal site to Drupal as migrating a non-Drupal site to Backdrop. For smaller sites, it may be easier to build it from scratch and migrate the content.

Summary

Migrating a Drupal 7 site to Backdrop is relatively straightforward but does require forethought and planning. The areas that are likely to cause the most effort in your migration efforts are contributed modules or themes that do not have a Backdrop equivalent or custom code or themes that you must manually port following the guidelines contained within this book. In either case, the vision and direction of the Backdrop team address the long-term needs of small to medium-sized organizations, and for those on Drupal 6, the time to migrate is now.

CHAPTER 9

■ ■ ■

Migrating to Backdrop from Drupal 6

Drupal 6 is quickly coming to its end of life as a supported platform. Drupal 8 has launched, meaning that the community's support for Drupal 6 will end on February 24, 2016. If you are an organization running on Drupal 6, you have two basic choices: continue to run your site on an unsupported platform and suffer the consequences of doing so or migrate your Drupal 6 site to Drupal 7, Drupal 8, or Backdrop.

If the decision is to migrate your site, the option to migrate to Drupal 7 provides you with a short-term solution that will at some point become unsupported like Drupal 6 has. Migrating to Drupal 8 is also an option; however, Drupal 8 brings with it several challenges for small to medium-sized organizations as the focus of Drupal 8 is on the requirements of larger enterprise-class organizations. The benefits of migrating to Backdrop are several, and many of those benefits are outlined throughout this book. However, there isn't a migration path from Drupal 6 to Backdrop without an intermediate step of migrating your Drupal 6 site to Drupal 7. This chapter walks you step by step through the process of migrating a Drupal 6 site, in preparation for either leaving your site on Drupal 7 or taking the additional step of moving to Backdrop. Regardless of the ultimate destination, you should still strongly consider moving off of Drupal 6.

Evaluating Your Drupal 6 Site

In preparation for the migration process, it is wise to evaluate your Drupal 6 site to identify any potential roadblocks that will prevent you from migrating your site. The following are specific things to examine:

- Look at the current state of the Drupal 6 contributed modules that your site utilizes. Check to see whether a Drupal 7 version of those modules exist and, if not, whether there are alternative solutions through other core or contributed modules. At this juncture, any Drupal 6 contributed module that is going to be ported to Drupal 7 will have already been ported. If there isn't a Drupal 7 version, you'll have to look elsewhere or forego the functionality provided by that module.

- Examine the functionality provided by custom modules that are used on your site and whether that functionality can be enabled through a Drupal 7 module. If not, you will be confronted with the task of porting your Drupal 6 module to Drupal 7 following the guidelines outlined at http://drupal.org/update/modules/6/7.

- Check out the current state of the Drupal 6 theme that your site utilizes. If you are using a Drupal 6 contributed theme, check to see whether there is a Drupal 7 equivalent. If not, the options are to select a different theme or port your Drupal 6 theme to Drupal 7 following the guidelines outlined at http://drupal.org/update/themes/6/7.

- After evaluating your inventory of modules and themes, you may determine that the effort to port your site would be better served by rebuilding your site from scratch in Backdrop and migrating the content on your site.

Preparing for the Migration to Drupal 7

If you choose to continue with migrating your site to Drupal 7 after evaluating the state of modules and theme used on your Drupal 6 site, the next steps will help you prepare your site:

1. Update to the latest version of Drupal 6.

2. Back up your existing site, including code, files, and database. Copy the backup to a safe place where it can't be deleted or modified.

3. Create a new temporary directory outside of your existing Drupal 6 site.

4. Download and extract the new version of Drupal 6 in your temporary directory. The unzip will likely create a directory named drupal-6.versionnumber where versionnumber represents the current minor release of Drupal 6.

5. Put your existing site into maintenance mode by visiting admin/settings/site-maintenance and choosing the appropriate options to set your site into maintenance mode.

6. Visit /admin/build/modules and write down all the noncore modules that you have enabled on your site (or take a screenshot).

7. Disable all the noncore modules that you have enabled.

8. Delete the sites/default/default.settings.php file on your existing site.

9.   Rename your `sites/default/settings.php` file to `sites/default/settings.old`.

10. Delete the `.htaccess` file in the root directory of the temporary Drupal 6 root directory.

11. Copy the content of your existing Drupal 6 installation's `sites` directory and all of its contents to the temporary root directory where you downloaded the latest version of Drupal 6.

12. In the temporary copy of Drupal 6's directory, copy the `default.settings.php` file in `sites/default` to `settings.php` and copy the database settings and any other configuration changes that you made that are found in the `settings.old` file to the `settings.php` file.

13. Copy the `.htaccess` and `robots.tx` files from the root directory of your existing site to the temporary copy of Drupal 6's root directory, overwriting the temporary Drupal 6 version of those files with your existing site's files.

14. Back up your old site and move the entire directory structure to a safe spot so that you can quickly restore the site should you run into issues during the update.

15. Copy the entire temporary copy of the latest version of Drupal 6, including your updates to `settings.php`, to the root folder of your Drupal 6 production site.

16. Run `update.php` on your site. Note If you are unable to run `update.php` without logging in, change the `$update_free_access` setting in `settings.php` to TRUE from FALSE. After changing it, you should be able to run `update.php` without logging in. After running `update.php`, remember to change the setting back to FALSE.

17. Log in to your site using an administrator's account and re-enable all the previously enabled modules.

18. Run `update.php` again to address any contributed module changes.

19. Back up your site, including code, files, and database.

20. Test your site to verify that everything is working.

21. Take your site out of maintenance mode by visiting `admin/settings/site-maintenance` and updating the appropriate values.

At this juncture, your site is now running the latest version of Drupal 6. The next step is to upgrade all the contributed modules to the latest version.

Upgrading Contributed Modules

With Drupal 6 core updated to the latest version, the next step in the process is to update all the contributed modules to their latest stable release. Visit `admin/reports/updates` and identify modules that need to be updated. If you find modules that are out of date, first evaluate whether the update will cause issues on your site.

- Check the module's documentation to see whether any patches were applied or customizations were made to the module for your specific site. While best practice is to make any changes to a module's functionality through a custom module that utilizes the contributed module's hooks, not all developers follow best practices, and there may be cases where someone has directly modified a module. If no apparent updates were made, you may want to compare the source of the same version of the module you have installed with the original source on Drupal.org for that module. If there were changes to a contributed module's source, you'll need to determine a path to ensure that the updated functionality is replicated in the newest version of that module.

- Read the module's documentation, typically the `READ.me` file, to see whether there are any constraints or conditions that may affect other modules. For example, an update to one module may impact another. If there are other modules that are affected, ensure that updating one module will not negatively impact the other related modules.

- Read the release notes for the newest version of the module. Check to see whether the update contains new features or bug fixes that are not critical to your web site. If they are not critical, you may choose to not update the module before migrating to Drupal 7.

- Check to see whether any of the changes are security related. Evaluate the criticality of the security flaw and determine whether your site is vulnerable. If not, you may choose to skip the update.

- Check the module's issue queue to see whether any new issues have been logged for the latest update. If so, determine whether those issues will impact your site.

If all looks well with the newest version of the module update it using the following steps:

1. Place your site in maintenance mode. Visit `/admin/settings/site-maintenance` and select the appropriate options.

2. Back up the site including the database.

3. Remove the existing module's files from within its root directory.

4. Download the latest version of the module and uncompress the files in the module's root folder.

5. Check /admin/build/modules to ensure that the new version of the module is recognized by your site and is enabled.

6. Check the status of your site by visiting /admin/reports/ status to see whether update.php needs to be run to update the schema of your database. If the report shows a pending database change, run /update.php.

7. Test the functionality provided by the new module. If all seems well, back up the site again and take the site out of maintenance mode.

8. Back up your site including code, files, and database.

With the Drupal 6 site upgraded to the current versions of core and contributed modules, it's time to begin the migration to Drupal 7.

Migrating the Drupal 6 Site to Drupal 7

Follow these steps:

1. Ensure that your Drupal 6 site is in maintenance mode by visiting /admin/settings/site-maintenance. If it is not in maintenance mode, put it back into maintenance mode.

2. Set your site's default theme to Garland by visiting /admin/ build/themes. Check the box for Enabled and the radio button for Default for the Garland theme. Disable any other themes by unchecking the Enabled check box. Click "Save configuration" at the bottom of the page to commit your changes to the database.

3. Disable all noncore and core optional modules by visiting /admin/build/modules.

4. If there are modules that are not available in Drupal 7, you may choose to uninstall them at this point. Click the Uninstall tab to view which modules may be uninstalled and click those you want to remove.

5. Delete the /sites/default/default.settings.php file on the Drupal 6 site.

6. Remove all old core files and directories outside the sites directory. If you made modifications to the .htaccess or robots.txt file, copy them to a safe place so they can be restored after the migration to Drupal 7.

7. If you uninstalled any modules, remove them from the /sites/all/modules directory, and in the case of a multisite installation, remove them from sites/*/modules. Leave all the other modules in place even though they are incompatible with Drupal 7.

8. Download the latest version of Drupal 7 from drupal.org/drupal to a directory outside your Drupal 6 installation. Extract and copy files contained within the Drupal 7 directory to your Drupal 6 directory.

9. If you made changes to .htaccess or robots.txt, copy those changes to the Drupal 7 version of those files.

10. Make your Drupal 6 version of /sites/default/settings.php writeable so that the update process can modify it to match the requirements for Drupal 7.

11. Run update.php by visiting /update.php. If you are unable to execute update.php, change $update_free_access in settings.php to TRUE and run /update.php. At the conclusion of executing update.php, change the value of $update_free_access back to FALSE.

12. Back up the site, including code, files, and database.

13. Update all your Drupal 6 contributed modules to Drupal 7 using the following steps for each module:

    a. Find the module on drupal.org/project/xxxxx where xxxx is the name of your module.

    b. Download the module to a temporary directory and extract it.

    c. Check the UPGRADE.txt files in each module to see whether any special upgrade instructions apply.

    d. Delete the Drupal 6 module's directory.

    e. Copy the temporary copy of the Drupal 7 module to /sites/all/modules.

    f. Enable the module at /admin/build/modules.

    g. Run update.php again and check for any errors.

    h. Examine any configuration values in the Drupal 7 version of the module by visiting the module's administration form, if one exists.

      i.   Test the functionality of the Drupal 7 version of the module.

      j.   Back up the database, code, and files after each module.

      k.   Continue the process with the next contributed module.

14.   Port your theme or find a Drupal 7 equivalent of your Drupal 6 theme.

15.   Replace functionality lost by modules that do not have a Drupal 6 equivalent. Use a Drupal 7 contributed module, use Drupal 7 core, or develop a custom solution.

16.   Update your settings.php file to the correct permissions so that it is protected.

17.   Unset maintenance mode to enable visitors to see the Drupal 7 version of your site.

It's likely that you'll encounter errors along the way of porting your Drupal 6 site to Drupal 7. There is a wealth of information on Drupal.org, and because of the community's efforts to port Drupal 6 to Drupal 7 over the past several years, it's likely that someone has already encountered the same or similar problems.

At this juncture you can decide whether to continue the process as described in Chapter 8 and port the Drupal 7 version of your site to Backdrop or remain on Drupal 7 for the foreseeable future.

Summary

Migrating a Drupal 6 site to Backdrop is a two-step process. You must first migrate from Drupal 6 to Drupal 7 and then, following the steps outlined in Chapter 8, from Drupal 7 to Backdrop. While it's a relatively straightforward process, there is work involved, and you'll likely hit a few bumps in the road. Don't give up if you do reach an error that is keeping you from reaching your goal. Check the Drupal community because there is a wealth of information and help freely available to all.

Good luck on your adventure in to Backdrop. It's an amazing platform with a vision that addresses a vast majority of organizations on the Web.

■ ■ ■

Contributing to Backdrop

The growth, adoption, and success of Backdrop require an active community that is contributing to Backdrop core, contributed modules, and themes. The Backdrop team has defined an easy-to-follow process for participating in the process. This appendix outlines the steps required to participate.

Core GitHub Workflow

All the code associated with Backdrop, including Backdrop core, contributed modules, and themes, are maintained on GitHub (http://github.com). To participate in the process, you'll need an account on GitHub, and you'll need to familiarize yourself with how GitHub works. Several resources are available on GitHub to guide you through the process of setting up git, creating repositories, forking repositories, and collaborating with others. I suggest spending a few minutes looking through the documentation on http://github.com before continuing.

Contributing to Backdrop Core

With an understanding of GitHub, you're ready to begin contributing to Backdrop. Visit http://github.com/backdrop/backdrop and create a new fork of Backdrop core in your own GitHub account. To create a fork, click the Fork icon at the top right of the page. For more information on forking a repository, visit http://help.github.com/articles/fork-a-repo/.

   With a copy of Backdrop core in your own repository, you are now ready to make the additions or changes that you want to contribute to the community. You can find a good source of opportunities to contribute to the issue queues at http://github.com/backdrop/backdrop-issues.

   When developing fixes or enhancements to Backdrop, make sure you are following Backdrop best practices as described on http://api.backdropcms.org/coding-standards. Always file an issue in the Backdrop Issue Tracker (http://github.com/backdrop/backdrop-issues) before you begin development to ensure that everyone knows what you're working on. When you've completed your development work, submit a pull request by clicking the "Pull requests" link in the right column of your fork's landing page.

Follow the steps as directed by GitHub to create the pull request, selecting "backdrop/backdrop" as the base fork and your fork as the head fork, and submit the request to the Backdrop project for review. (Note: Pull requests will be closed immediately if they do not have a corresponding issue in the Backdrop issue tracker.) Include a descriptive sentence in your commit message describing what your commit accomplished and the Backdrop Issue Tracker number, trying to keep it to a single sentence. A maintainer or fellow contributor should then review the changes and ensure tests pass. If everything looks good, the code will be merged into the main project by a committer.

Trouble with Tests?

The core Backdrop repository on GitHub incorporates automated testing using Travis CI. All pull requests will be automatically tested and a report submitted suggesting whether the pull request has passed all tests or which tests failed. If you're encountering regular failures when submitting pull requests, you can use multiple approaches to resolve the test failures without needing to make pull requests.

- Run the tests locally. You can run tests locally by enabling the SimpleTest module and then visiting `admin/config/development/testing` and running the individual test that failed.

- Run the tests using the shell script. If you're running all the tests, you may benefit from using the shell script version of the test suite, which can run faster by executing tests in parallel. To do this, enable the SimpleTest module on your site, and then using a command line at the root of your Backdrop installation, run this command:

```
./core/scripts/run-tests.sh --concurrency 8 --url 'http://localhost/' --all
```

▓ **Note**   You'll need to replace `localhost` with the URL of your installation.

- Enable Travis CI on your GitHub repository. Travis CI can run the test suite for you without needing to file a pull request; simply sign into Travis CI at `http://travis-ci.org` (via OAuth using your Github credentials), visit your profile on Travis CI, and enable testing on your fork of Backdrop. Now Travis CI will test every commit you make to your repository! For details on how to set up Travis CI, visit `http://docs.travis-ci.com/user/for-beginners`.

Making Clean Pull Requests

If you make a lot of commits to your repository branch while trying to fix tests or solve other problems, it's a good idea to clean up your commits before filing a pull request. Because your commit history will be merged directly into the parent project, each commit message should be clear about its purpose. Having complete commit messages makes examining the history with the git log and git blame commands easier.

Here are the things to avoid in pull requests:

- An excessive number of commits (usually, more than one)

- Debugging or test commits

- Poorly formatted commit messages, a missing "Issue #xxx: " prefix, or more than one line in length

If you've made a pull request that needs cleaning up, it's easy to solve this problem by deleting the pull request, fixing the commits locally, and then making a new pull request. Let's assume you had filed a pull request on the branch with the name my_branch; you could clean up its commits with the following commands:

- Rebase all your changes to move them to the top of the commit log using git rebase 1.x

- For more information about git rebase visit git-scm.com/docs/git-rebase.

- Edit the last five commits together with an interactive rebase: git rebase -i HEAD~5.

This will open your default text editor with an interface like this:

text

```
pick f6dcf28 blah
pick 0ee28af Issue #77: Removing further files[] instances from .info files.
pick 22ade13 issue 77: Removing registry building from SimpleTest.
pick 9e33534 debugging
pick c5f376b 77 Fixing incorrect path to filetransfer classes

# Rebase 1e5974e..c5f376b onto 1e5974e
#
# Commands:
# p, pick = use commit
# r, reword = use commit, but edit the commit message
# e, edit = use commit, but stop for amending
# s, squash = use commit, but meld into previous commit
# f, fixup = like "squash", but discard this commit's log message
# x, exec = run command (the rest of the line) using shell
#
# If you remove a line here THAT COMMIT WILL BE LOST.
# However, if you remove everything, the rebase will be aborted
```

To combine these commits into a single commit, change the word *pick* to *fixup* (or just *f* for short). At the same time, you can change the overall commit message by modifying the first commit and changing it to *reword* (or *r* for short). You can leave all the lines that start with a hash sign; they won't affect your rebase.

```
reword f6dcf28 Issue #77: Replacing the registry with a more reliable
alternative.
f 0ee28af Issue #77: Removing further files[] instances from .info files.
f 22ade13 issue 77: Removing registry building from SimpleTest.
f 9e33534 debugging
f c5f376b 77 Fixing incorrect path to filetransfer classes
```

This will take all five commits and combine them into a single commit with a clean message. If you make any mistakes, just close your editor and use `git rebase --abort` to cancel the rebasing.

Now with all the commits nicely merged together, you can push your branch to GitHub a second time and file the pull request again with the new, cleaner commit messages. You'll have to "force" push the changes to overwrite your current pull request: `git push origin my_branch -f`.

Contribute to a Module, Layout, or Theme

If you've created a module or theme for Backdrop CMS, we encourage you to collaborate with others in improving and maintaining it. All new modules for Backdrop CMS should be hosted on GitHub.

Join the Backdrop Contrib group on GitHub by submitting an issue to the Backdrop Contributed Module Issue Queue. The queue is monitored for new applicants. After being accepted, you will be able to create a new project (or move an existing one) under the Backdrop Contrib group at `http://github.com/backdrop-contrib`.

Contributing to an Existing Project

The process for contributed projects is similar to that for Backdrop core and involves the following:

- Forking the repository on GitHub into your own account

- Cloning the repository to your own computer

- Modifying the code

- Committing and pushing the code to your repository

- Making a pull request back to the original project

In this case, however, automated testing is not likely to be available, so it is even more important to ensure that you are submitting quality code. If the project you are contributing to includes tests, it is best to run these in your browser locally by enabling the SimpleTest module and then visiting admin/config/development/testing and running the individual tests.

Courtesy in Contributing Code

Note that all contributors to Backdrop projects are added to the "authors" group of the "Backdrop CMS contributed projects" repository, which means that anyone, once granted initial permission, has access to modify projects being maintained by other authors. This is an issue with GitHub's permission system and for now cannot be avoided. Backdrop's contributors are asked not to directly modify projects being maintained by others without first establishing contact and obtaining the go-ahead from the contrib maintainer.

Contributed Development Branches

Contrib branches should reflect the core major version (1.x) followed by a hyphen and then your module's major version (1.x). For example, 1.x-2.x indicates it is the 2.x version of a module made for Backdrop 1.x.

Contributed Releases

When making official releases of your project on GitHub, please follow the same semantic versioning patterns used by Backdrop core but also include a prefix indicating the version of Backdrop core in which the project is compatible. Contrib release tags should include the core major version followed by a hyphen and then your module's major.minor. patch number. For example 1.x-1.0.0 indicates it is the 1.0.0 release of a project that is compatible with Backdrop 1.x. See the devel module releases for a real-world example.

APPENDIX B

■ ■ ■

Additional Resources

There is a growing list of resources available for those who are interested in Backdrop.
This appendix contains the primary places to begin your search for more information.

- *Issue Queue, GitHub*: The primary means of communication is
  the Backdrop Issue queue at http://github.com/backdrop/
  backdrop-issues/issues.This is where all the discussion
  happens around adding new features or fixing bugs.

- *API documentation and change records*. You can find all the
  Backdrop APIs at http://api.backdropcms.org. The API web
  site contains the list of public functions, hooks, and subsystem
  documentation. It also contains all the changes documenting
  differences between Drupal 7 and Backdrop.

- *Weekly meetings, Google Hangouts*: Backdrop holds weekly
  meetings on Thursdays at 1 p.m. Pacific time. These are
  open meetings that anyone can join; visit Google Plus at
  http://plus.google.com/+BackdropcmsOrg to join in.

- *Video archives, YouTube*: All weekly meetings are recorded and
  published to the YouTube channel at www.youtube.com/user/
  backdropcms. This channel is also home to tutorial videos on
  contributing to and using the Backdrop CMS.

- *Reddit*: Discuss with the Backdrop community at the Backdrop
  CMS subredit found at http://reddit.com/r/backdrop.

- *Live chat, IRC*: Backdrop has an official IRC channel on
  http://irc.freenode.net at #backdrop.

- *Twitter*: Backdrop has an official Twitter account: @backdropcms.

- *Facebook*: Backdrop has an official Facebook page at
  http://facebook.com/backdropcms.

Index

Get the eBook for only $5!

Why limit yourself?

Now you can take the weightless companion with you wherever you go and access your content on your PC, phone, tablet, or reader.

Since you've purchased this print book, we're happy to offer you the eBook in all 3 formats for just $5.

Convenient and fully searchable, the PDF version enables you to easily find and copy code—or perform examples by quickly toggling between instructions and applications. The MOBI format is ideal for your Kindle, while the ePUB can be utilized on a variety of mobile devices.

To learn more, go to www.apress.com/companion or contact support@apress.com.

Printed in the United States
By Bookmasters